flash in the pan

flash in the pan

what to cook, and how

Tushita Patel

westland

westland ltd

571, Poonamallee High Road, Kamaraj Bhavan, Aminijikarai, Chennai 600 029
No.38/10 (New No.5), Raghava Nagar, New Timber Yard Layout, Bangalore 560 026
Survey No. A - 9, II Floor, Moula Ali Industrial Area, Moula Ali, Hyderabad 500 040
Plot No 102, Marol Coop Ind Estate, Marol, Andheri East, Mumbai 400 059
47, Brij Mohan Road, Daryaganj, New Delhi 110 002

First published by westland ltd 2009

Copyright © Tushita Patel 2009

All rights reserved

10 9 8 7 6 5 4 3 2 1

ISBN: 978-93-80032-64-1

EDITED BY Sherna Wadia

BOOK DESIGN Akshay Raj Singh Rathore

PRINTED AT Thomson Press, New Delhi

This book is sold subject to the condition that it shall not by way of trade or otherwise, be lent, resold, hired out, circulated, and no reproduction in any form, in whole or in part (except for brief quotations in critical articles or reviews) may be made without written permission of the publishers.

contents

Introduction vii

Finger Food 1
Show Dinners 23
Soul Dinners 63
Weekday Eating 93
Before and After 115
Cool Kitchen Essentials 133

Index 139

introduction

Someone asked me once the question so favoured by lifestyle magazines: If there was one food you had to eat every day, what would it be?

I think because I didn't have an answer, or because I have always been so spoilt for choice, I answered: Cyanide.

I am from a generation that has had the good fortune of travelling with friends who like to impress by finding amazing restaurants or cooking fabulous meals. We learnt what we liked to eat, where you could get it and, about the time Google became verb from noun, how to cook it.

The chapters in this book are in keeping with how we live. During the week, most people meet for a drink as dinners are too intense, both for the host who may have to cook, and the perpetual weekday eater (dieter). Drinks is easy – suddenly, local booze shops are stocked with a huge range of spirits and wines, but when it comes to the 'eats' with the drinks (known as bitings or munchings in certain semi-urban quarters), we just open a packet of chips or peanuts. Or we order kababs. In Finger Food, I have tried to keep it simple, cool and slightly sexy – with the option of opening packets, but something that's not just peanuts. I have suggested bhakri (baked Gujarati biscuits) and boursin (creamy cheese available everywhere these days) in the cheese platter – oh, I have been serving diced aam papad with cheese to great success. There's super easy and super elegant steamed shrimps dipped in Japanese soy sauce, to slightly labour-intensive, but most marvellous beef and lettuce wraps. I like retro food and believe in feeding the soul – and my soul is fed after a plate of deep-fried, politically-incorrect chilli cheese toasts.

The big entertaining happens over weekends. This is the core of the book – I believe in playing to the galleries with flashy cooking that will generate oohs and aahs and some envy, not necessarily comfort food (at a party) and mother's cooking. I also believe in working less – so this chapter is really about how to make an impression with minimal effort. A pork raja mircha with boiled vegetables or cold sesame noodles is very statement cooking. When you serve khowswey, it's victory of the idea over the food (which is fab too). What's not to like when guests stand around the table and stare at the food in admiration, then go on to polish bowls of it in a steamy blur?

On days you don't want to make a statement, but still eat well or share a meal, there is what I call Soul Dinners. A kadhi can evoke memories of home cooking, but sexed up with garlic, it becomes something quite wicked. After long workdays, I could feel like a hot dal-chawal-fried egg, but on a lot of days I sit in front of the TV eating fried potatoes and bacon on white bread, not because I'm particularly suicidal, but it's so irresistible. There's wicked joy in sharing this recipe.

The Weekday Eating Chapter is the opposite of suicide – it is about trying to be good and eat healthy. I have tried to do things here from traditional Bengali and other Indian home cooking. Things that are often eaten as a side dish which I have tried to turn around to make meals out of them. I love eating boiled pumpkin drizzled with glistening mustard oil out of my lunch box, sitting in front of my computer screen, sucking up the sweet pumpkin, the sharpness of the mustard and flecks of hot green chilli. I hardly ever have salad days, but when I do, I work at sprucing them up with healthy things like anchovies and garlic, and try and walk away from those I love – mayo and olive oil (litres of it is not healthy).

I have admitted that I don't know enough desserts to fill a chapter, so I have tried to camouflage it with drinks – which I pride myself for knowing a thing or two about. I like surprises, and while drinking at drinking time is all right, I love it when I unexpectedly finish work early and there's a chance to gather around a cold pitcher of sangria and watch the sunset from my friend's terrace. One of my favourite drinks moments is in Goa, during breakfast after an early morning swim at a shack. It's hard to drink a glass of fresh orange or watermelon juice or tender coconut water, sitting on a beach early in the morning, and not have a shot of vodka in it. Generations of shack-owners have indulged me with my early morning drink.

While we are on the kindness of strangers, indulge me in the Kitchen Essentials Chapter – a completely arbitrary list of what I think is important in a kitchen. It's easy to dismiss candied orange peel, but on days when you have nothing but vanilla ice-cream in the freezer, this is what will elevate you from just vanilla to a sublime sundae.

This book is for those who have access to good ingredients and not afraid to try. A flash in the pan is better than never having done it.

Tushita Patel

table of measures

1 cup = 200 ml
1 tsp = 5 ml
1 tbsp = 3 tsp

A pinch = ⅛ tsp (literally a pinch)
A dash = 1-2 drops

All spoon and cup measures are level unless otherwise indicated

finger food

I thought of calling this chapter Starters, but dropped the idea. Wouldn't that imply the appearance of Enders?

Finger food is a means to its own end – lots of small things that come and go, each generating a wow – either in the way it looks, tastes, or is put together. Sometimes all three.

This book is all about keeping it deceptive – simple yes, but stylish and flashy.

Most people I know do drinks at bars. Only a few would prepare a menu, which is somewhat original (if they don't want India's two favourite cocktail snacks – chicken reshmi kabab and baby corn Manchurian), shop for quality ingredients, do a reasonable amount of prep, and then put it together.

Those who can muster the confidence of calling people home for drinks (which also implies nibbly bits), exude a hint of sexiness and promise.

I often make a pitcher of sangria and call some people over around sunset. Before they walk into the kitchen and start searching for jars to open and munch, I try and serve something.

Easy Bruschetta Platter

For 12-14 bruschetta

Bruschetta (pronounced broos-keta) is Italy's gift to the world of dazzling starters. It could be as easy as toasting bread, as that is what the word means – toasted bread – rub with garlic, drizzle with olive oil; or it could be jazzed up depending on what you have at home or what your guests like. A platter of these can take care of varied food preferences. The only note of caution is that they have to be eaten almost as soon as they come out of the kitchen, or they turn soggy. Also, this is the dish for you to use the expensive extra virgin olive oil if you have it. Serve it on a big plate or a platter, or even a tray. Colour coordinate according to the toppings for extra oohs.

(Quick calculator: Average bruschetta consumption during a two- to three-hour party would be four per person)

Basic Bruschetta

Baguette or multi-grained bread, sliced (at a pinch, white bread) – 1
Garlic – 2 cloves
Extra virgin olive oil – about 1 tsp per slice

Grill the slices in an oven on both sides or toast to a crusty golden in a toaster.

While the bread is being heated, cut each garlic clove diagonally into two.

Gently take the toasts out of the hot oven.

While they are still hot, rub the cut end of the garlic slices on the bread. You might want to keep the oven mitts on while you're doing this.

With a generous hand, swirl the bottle of olive oil over the toasts. The idea is for the bread to absorb the flavour of the (good) olive oil.

This can be eaten in itself. It is one of my own favourite midnight TV snacks, if you can handle the garlic breath. Otherwise pile on any of the toppings given in the following pages.

Tomato & Basil Topping

Tomatoes, not too ripe, chopped – 3
Basil, roughly torn – a handful/3 tbsp + extra for garnish
Garlic, minced – 2 cloves
Black pepper, freshly ground – to taste
Parmesan, grated – 3 tbsp
Extra virgin olive oil – as much as you like

Mix the tomatoes, basil and garlic in a bowl.

Grind the pepper and grate the Parmesan generously into the bowl and toss.

Top off with some large glugs of olive oil.

Cover with cling film and refrigerate for at least an hour.

When guests arrive, spoon the topping on to the bruschetta.

Tear some more fresh basil, sprinkle on top and serve immediately.

Roasted Bell Pepper Topping

Red bell peppers – 2
Yellow bell peppers – 2
Garlic, finely chopped – 2 cloves
Thyme – 2 sprigs
Salt – ½ tsp
Olive oil – as much as you like

Chargrill the bell peppers over a flame or under a grill, turning them around till the skins are uniformly black and blistered.

Put them in a paper bag and close. Keep them in for 5 minutes to sweat; then peel the skin off neatly.

With a sharp knife, scoop out the top, and pull out the seeds.

Chop the bell peppers, add the garlic, thyme and salt and mix, stirring in the olive oil.

Pile on to the bruschetta and serve.

Runny Eggs Topping

Oil – 1 tsp
Butter or ghee – 1 tsp
Onion, small, finely chopped – 1
Green or bird chillies, finely chopped – 2
Tomato, small, finely chopped – 1
Eggs – 6
Salt – ½ tsp
Garam masala powder – ½ tsp
Coriander leaves, chopped – 2 tbsp

Heat the oil in a pan, add the butter or ghee. When it melts, add the onion and chillies and cook on moderate heat. Once the onions turn translucent, add the tomato and let it soften.

Beat the eggs with salt in a bowl.

Sprinkle the garam masala into the pan, give it all a quick stir and pour in the eggs, stirring it moderately till it takes solid form.

Turn off the heat at this point and take the pan off the hob. The trick of this dish is consistency – it should be slightly runny.

Mix a generous amount of chopped coriander leaves.

Spoon on to the bruschetta and serve.

This lends itself to many variations:

- With just plain eggs. (Delhi Press Club serves runny scrambled eggs on deep-fried, crispy bread – so decadent.)
- Or with egg and grated cheese.
- In Surat, I ate the runniest eggs with tender green garlic shoot at its Khau Galli.
- Chives are great too.
- For the simpler toppings, don't use ghee. Oil or butter is good enough.

Boiled Egg Bhurji Topping

This is my husband, Aakar's, speciality … my Sunday breakfast-in-bed treat. I sit around in a pile of Sunday newspapers, eating these colourful eggs on crunchy toast, dropping breadcrumbs on the sheets, followed by a cup (or two) of lemongrass tea (page 116). I have tweaked it and served it at parties as finger food to the minor wonderment of guests at its simplicity.

Oil – 1 tbsp
Onion, medium-sized, finely chopped – 1
Tomato, large, finely chopped – 1
Coriander powder – ½ tsp
Cumin powder – ½ tsp
Chilli powder – ½ tsp
Turmeric powder – ½ tsp
Salt – ½ tsp or more
Boiled eggs, slightly runny – 4
Coriander leaves, chopped – 2 tbsp

Heat the oil in a pan, add the onion and cook on moderate heat till the edges start turning slightly brown.

Mix in the tomatoes and cook till soft.

Sprinkle in the spice powders and salt and cook for a minute. Turn off the heat.

Chop the boiled eggs roughly and gently mix it with the rest of the ingredients in the pan. A soft touch is important here; you don't want to mash the eggs. It's important to retain the various textures.

Sprinkle in coriander leaves and serve on buttered baguette slices.

Mushroom Topping

Olive oil – 1 tsp
Garlic, finely chopped – 2 cloves
Sliced mushrooms – 2 cups
Thyme – 2 sprigs
Black pepper, freshly ground – to taste
Lime juice – 1 tsp
Salt (if not using Parmesan) – ¼ tsp
Grated Parmesan (optional) – up to 1 tsp per bruschetta

Heat the oil in a pan on moderate heat. Add the garlic. It will turn golden in less than a minute.

Toss in the mushrooms and stir and cook till they wilt and stop letting off moisture.

Take the pan off the heat, mix in the rest of the ingredients except the salt and Parmesan.

Hold back the salt if you are using Parmesan, else taste and add it.

Pile on to the bruschetta, sprinkle with Parmesan if being used, and serve.

Bacon and Potato Topping

Potatoes, large – 2/250 gms
Salt – 1 tsp
Olive oil – 1 tbsp
Bacon – 250 gms
Flat leaf parsley, chopped – 2 tbsp

Boil the potatoes in 2 litres of water with the salt for 7-8 minutes. Peel them and dice into small cubes.

Heat the oil in a heavy-based pan. Turn the heat to moderate.

Chop the bacon into squares and add it to the pan. This should cook slowly for around 10 minutes, oozing fat and shrinking in the process.

Raise the heat. Toss in the potatoes and give the pan a good shake so that they turn slightly crusty and golden on the outside.

Turn the heat down and cook for another 10 minutes.

With a slotted spoon, empty the contents of the pan on to layers of heavy-duty paper towels.

Sprinkle the chopped parsley on the bacon and potatoes.

Spoon on to hot bruschetta and serve quickly. No fun eating it all congealed.

(Not for those on the Atkins or any other diet.)

Prawn Cocktail

For 4

When my parents got married, my mother couldn't boil an egg. My father, a progressive man in many ways, sent her to the Catering College (now the Institute of Hotel Management) where she learnt to cook what was then known as Continental food. On the days she had classes, she came home with the dishes she learnt – fish mayonnaise, roast chicken, mulligatawny soup, fish meunière, chicken a la Kiev. My parents would sit for dinner on a small round table and eat these exotic dishes. I was either conceived as a result of these meals, or she was already expecting me during this period. I have mayo flowing in my veins.

The cold, creamy, fishy, tangy, sharp and sweet prawn cocktail is the jewel in her crown. She, of course, makes her own mayo (page 136).

Shelled prawns – 300 gms
Salt – ¼ tsp
Chilli powder – ½ tsp
Mayonnaise – 1 cup
Tomato ketchup – 8 tbsp
Cream – 4 tbsp
Tabasco sauce – a few drops

De-vein, clean and wash the prawns in several changes of water.

Heat a cup of water in a pan, add the prawns, salt and chilli powder and simmer on gentle heat for around 5 minutes – just till the prawns turn opaque and lose their pinkness.

Take the pan off the heat. Cool naturally.

Mix all the other ingredients in a bowl. The colour of the sauce will be pink. Taste as you go along. Some people prefer less ketchup, some like more Tabasco.

Add the prawns along with a 1-2 tbsp of the cooking liquid. Refrigerate for at least 4 hours.

My mother serves her prawn cocktail in martini glasses as a first course at her dinner parties. I like to serve mine on melba toast.

Melba Toast

Thinly slice a French loaf or a baguette. Bake in the oven preheated to 150°C till the slices turn slightly golden and curl up a bit in the heat.

Cool and store in an airtight container.

Shami Kabab

For 25-30 kababs

A colleague in Delhi used to bring these in her lunch box during Ramzan, to eat at Iftar after her prayers. Those of us for whom there is no bigger religion than food, found it hard to control ourselves once she made the mistake of sharing it with us. These kababs melt in the mouth like pâté, leaving a spicy, aromatic and hot aftertaste. Big hit at all parties.

Minced lamb, ideally fatty – 500 gms
Husked chana dal, soaked overnight – ½ cup
Onions, large, chopped – 2
Ginger, roughly chopped – ½-inch piece
Garlic – 4 cloves
Dried red chillies – 6
Black cardamoms – 2
Cinnamon – 2-inch stick
Cloves – 4
Salt – 2 tsp
Oil for deep frying – 1 cup
Onions, sliced – 2

Use your hands to mix (almost knead) the mince, dal, chopped onions, ginger, garlic, chillies, whole spices and salt.

Pressure-cook the mince mixture without water on low heat for 20 minutes. Turn off the heat and cool.

In batches, blend the entire mixture till it becomes a smooth, pliable dough.

Heat the oil for deep frying.

Fry the sliced onions (in batches, if the pan is not large enough for the onions to float) till crisp and golden. Sprinkle some water while frying the onions. (I recently got this tip from an old Bengali cookbook. Was pleasantly surprised to see it worked: the onions turned out uniformly golden and crunchy.)

Drain on double-layered paper towels.

Mix the fried onions with the mince dough.

Heat a non-stick frying pan and put in about ½ tbsp of oil to grease the surface.

Roll the dough into balls the size of small lemons and flatten them a bit so that they sit on the pan. Fry each side till a crust forms.

Serve with lime wedges, chopped mint leaves and onion rings. Or with my basic party dip (page 13).

Shami Sandwich

For 1 sandwich

Use leftover kababs to make sandwiches for a midnight snack or in a packed lunch.

White bread slices - 2
Butter - *if you like*
Mint chutney
Lettuce leaves (optional)
Shami kababs - 2

Trim off the bread crusts, butter the slices, if you like, followed by some mint chutney.

If you are feeling virtuous, line the slices with a leaf of lettuce.

Place the 2 kababs on a bread slice, flatten slightly with your hand and cover with the second slice.

Cut the sandwich diagonally, wrap in paper towel, put into a lunch box.

If you don't have mint chutney, tomato sauce or mustard and an onion ring are a good substitute.

Chicken and Wasabi Buns

For 6

I have a vague recollection of eating something in a bun at a noodle bar in New York. I think I overdid the sake – can't quite remember what exactly it was, but just a warm feeling which involved a small bun, wasabi mayo and perhaps roast beef. I tried to recreate what I recalled, at home. I replaced the beef with chicken, not because of any culinary reason, but because there was some chicken at home.

The trick is to source good buns – wholewheat is good, or in our case in Bandra, we use poi, Goan buns fermented with arrack. Remember, this is only a starter and should not resemble big brother hamburger in any form. If you don't get small enough buns, just cut them in half before serving. Should look elegant. Let some of the mayo show against the dark green rocket. People are impressed.

Chicken on the bone – 750 gms
Parsley, finely chopped – 2 tbsp
Salt – ½ tsp
Black pepper, freshly ground – 1 tsp
Onion, small, chopped – 1
Mayonnaise – 2 tbsp
Wasabi – ½ tsp or more if you like
Buns – 6
Rocket leaves (optional) – 12

Simmer the chicken, parsley, salt, pepper and onion along with a cup of water for 20-25 minutes in a covered pan on moderate heat.

Once cool, place the chicken in the stock, covered, in the refrigerator for 1-2 hour (or more is fine).

Before serving, extract the chicken from the stock. Don't throw away the stock. Strain and refrigerate. There will be other recipes (yes, in this book too) where you could use it.

Pull the chicken off the bones.

Mix the mayo and the wasabi into the chicken. Most of my guests are masochistic wasabi eaters and it's a pleasure to indulge them, but if your guests are not used to having a weird sensation in their nostrils, stick to the ½ tsp.

Slit the bun in half as you would for a burger. Put in a couple of leaves of rocket, if you like, and a generous filling of the chicken.

If the buns are too big, cut in half and serve.

Sometimes, I like to toast the buns a bit under the grill for about 7 minutes and then add the filling. There's the crunch of the bun against the cool softness of the meat followed by a wasabi kick. Only compliments thereafter.

Works well with leftover roast chicken, beef or pork too.

Hot Chilli Pork in a Bun

For 6

This dish is the antithesis of the one before; if that is cool and soothing, this is robust and in-your-face. No fun for those who can't do chillies, or pork fat. It is slightly gooey with the melted fat, the strong soy and hot chillies.

Pork, cubed, 20 per cent fat recommended – *400 gms*
Dark soy sauce – *½ cup*
Green chillies, finely chopped – *3*
Bird chillies, finely chopped – *3*
Oil – *2 tsp*
Small buns – *6*

Marinate the pork in the soy and chillies for at least 2 hours (6 is optimum).

Heat the oil in a heavy-based pan and pour in the pork with its marinade. Stir and cook for a minute on high heat.

Lower the heat to moderate and cook for 20 minutes. The fat and juices from the pork should have run by now, and the meat become tender.

Raise the heat and cook for 2 minutes to dry it up a bit if you like.

Slit the buns, fill them with the pork and serve.

Better warm than cold.

Chilli Potatoes

For 5

Potatoes, medium-sized – 4
Soy sauce – 4 tbsp
Green chillies, finely chopped – 3
Bird chillies, finely chopped – 3
Salt – ½ tsp
Oil – 3 tbsp
Onion, sliced – 1

Peel and dice the potatoes and wash in several changes of water till the water runs clear. Soak it in iced water while you complete the rest of the prep.

Drain the potatoes, pat dry with paper towels and put them in a bowl.

Pour in the soy sauce, chillies and salt and marinate the potatoes for as long as you can. Even 20 minutes is fine.

When you're ready to eat, heat the oil in a pan.

When smoking, put in the onion and cook on high heat till the edges start to brown.

With a slotted spoon, take the potatoes out of the marinade and add them to the hot pan.

Stir on high heat for 1-2 minutes, then turn down the heat. Let the oil bubble away. In about 8-10 minutes, the potatoes will be done. Poke one with a knife to check: it should go through easily but the potato should still give some resistance.

Pour the marinade into the pan, turn the heat back to high and cook for 3-4 minutes. The liquid will reduce and thicken, infusing the potatoes with an intense soy flavour and the heat of the chillies.

Pour into a serving dish and serve with toothpicks.

Five (Skinny) Dips

Dips are easy and elegant, and hold out promise for the rest of the evening – a big impression with minimal effort. I make my basic dip by turning over a tub of yogurt on to a strainer lined with muslin, and suspending the whole thing over a bowl in the refrigerator till I get back from work. By then, it's creamy and cold. Depending on my mood, I beat it up with salt and any or all of: garlic paste, chopped spring onion, chilli flakes, dill. When I feel posh, it's just freshly ground black pepper (and salt) – it's like eating boursin cheese, especially if the yogurt is set thick.

I serve this with plain Gujarati bhakri – flaky baked discs that I buy from the grocery store; crackers too.

Even ordinary dips like these allow a sense of drama in the presentation. A vegetable platter can provide the colours to offset the creamy whiteness of the dip – radishes (especially the small red ones in season), carrots, celery, cucumber. Else there are golden fried potato chips, which never last long enough for anyone to admire their beauty. Speaking of potatoes, a dip and roast potato is a match made in gastro heaven. You could half-boil the potatoes in their skins. Dry, toss them in a bit in olive oil and salt, bung into the oven and grill on high for about 12 minutes. Hot, crusty potatoes, smeared in cold dip are a thing of beauty.

Basic Party Dip

For 8

Yogurt – *400 gms*
Olive oil – *2 tbsp*
Chopped dill – *3 tbsp*
Garlic, crushed – *2 cloves*
Chilli flakes – *1 tsp*
Salt – *to taste*

Pour the yogurt into a strainer lined with clean muslin cloth or a handkerchief over a bowl for at least 6 hours, ideally in the refrigerator.

Discard the whey, and pour the yogurt into a big, deep bowl.

Mix in all other ingredients and give it a good whisk.

Pour into a serving bowl or several small bowls and serve with chopped vegetables, crisps or even on Monaco biscuits, artily squeezed out with an icing cone.

If you don't have dill, you can do crushed garlic and freshly ground black pepper – make sure the pepper is not too fine. For me, just plain garlic is good enough too.

finger food

A Version of Guacamole

For 8

Avocado – 2 ripe
Blue or Gorgonzola cheese, grated – 2 tbsp
Spring onion, chopped – 2 tbsp
Garlic, finely chopped – 1 small clove
Chilli powder – ½ tsp
Lime juice – 1 tsp
Salt – ½ tsp

Most avocados are ready for a salad when the skin is black. Some varieties, however, never turn black. The trick is to shake the fruit: if you can hear the seed rattle, and the flesh is firm to the touch, it is ready.

To take out the flesh, run the knife around the equator of the avocado, twist and pull out the half. Scoop the flesh out with a spoon and mash it. Take out the seed and mash the other half.

Add all other ingredients and mix it up smoothly.

Serve with tortilla chips.

Hot and Sour Dip

For 4

Tomatoes – 2
Red chillies – 2 or more if you like
Tabasco sauce – a few drops or more
Garlic – 4 cloves
Sea salt – 1 tsp
Extra virgin olive oil – 3 tbsp

Chargrill the tomatoes over a flame or under the grill till the skin is uniformly black and blistered. Keep them inside a paper bag for 5 minutes to sweat, and peel off the skin.

Put the tomatoes, with the rest of the ingredients in a blender and blitz.

Serve with nachos or corn chips.

Tapenade

For 5

Pitted black olives in brine – 1 cup
Garlic – 1 clove
Olive oil – 3 tbsp

Coarsely pulse-grind the olives and garlic in a blender.

Empty into a bowl (white looks nice, contrasting the dark purple of the olives).

Make some tracks on the surface with a fork and pour olive oil into them.

Guests can either dunk pieces of crusty bread into this, or spread some on bruschetta.

Hummus

For 6

Boiled chickpeas – 2 cups
Garlic – 5 cloves
Tahini/sesame paste – 2 tbsp
Lime juice – 2 tbsp
Salt – ½ tsp
Extra virgin olive oil – 2 tbsp
Chilli powder – 1 tsp
Parsley, chopped – 2 tbsp

Grind the boiled chickpeas with at least 4 tbsp of its cooking liquid and the garlic, tahini, lime juice and salt. You may need to add more of the cooking liquid to get the consistency right. It should be runny like cake batter, but slightly grainy.

Pour this into a bowl and run the tines of a fork to furrow through it. Pour some olive oil on top to make puddles, sprinkle with chilli powder and chopped parsley.

Serve with pita bread. It's nice as a topping for bruschetta too.

Good olive oil can lift a hummus from good to sublime, so save the good oil for this.

Club Chilli Cheese Toast

For 4 toasts

White bread slices – 2
Green chilli, minced – 1
Amul or Cheddar cheese, grated – 3 tbsp
Butter – for the toast

Turn the grill on to high.

Butter the bread and cut the slices diagonally.

Mix the chilli into the cheese and spoon this generously on the bread.

Put the slices on a baking tray or an ovenproof dish and grill for 8-10 minutes.

Serve with tomato ketchup or hot garlic sauce.

Politically-Incorrect Chilli Cheese Toast

For 36 toasts

These we used to eat when we didn't know better – there's always a price for something so spectacular.

White bread slices – 6
Oil – to cover base of pan by ½ inch
Egg yolk – 1
Chilli powder – 1 tsp
Amul cheese, grated – ¾ cup

Trim the crusts of the bread slices and discard. Cut each slice through the length into 3 pieces. Cut each length into half to get 6 pieces.

Put the oil in a frying pan on moderate heat.

Beat the egg yolk in a bowl, add the chilli powder and the cheese and beat it with a fork till it is a slightly runny, golden yellow emulsion.

Drop dollops of this on the bread.

The oil should have warmed by now, but not smoking.

Gently lower each of these cheese-covered toasts into the oil with the bread side down and lower the heat.

As soon as the bread starts changing colour (this will be in less than a minute), turn them over one by one, using tongs. By the time you finish turning all of them, it will be time to take them out on to a bed of double-lined paper towels.

Once drained, serve with hot sauce.

The trick in this is to control the temperature of the oil so that the bread doesn't get burnt, and beat the egg and cheese a bit to incorporate air so that the cheesy top resembles a pillow.

Cheese Plus Plus

A cheese platter is tricky. While it raises the bar at a party, there are some who are repulsed by smelly cheeses. Thankfully, the majority of my guests love it when I serve interesting cheeses that I get from the fancy deli at my local market. The thing to remember is what people are drinking. Spirits like whisky or vodka clash violently with cheese, while wine and cheese are … wine and cheese.

Boursin and Bhakri
For 6

Boursin is a creamy cheese, which comes in several flavours like garlic, pepper, chives and so on. My favourite is pepper. I stumbled across this Franco-Gujarati combination by accident. The shop where I was buying the cheese was a Kathiawadi-owned grocery store, which keeps all kinds of exotic imported goodies, along with Gujarati staples like thepla and khakra. Bhakri are baked flaky discs, which also come in flavours – garlic, cumin, masala and so on.

I bought the cheese to serve at a party and the bhakri to serve separately. After a point, some of the guests started breaking off bits of bhakri to scoop up the pliable cheese. A classic combo was born.

Unwrap the boursin from its mould and serve it on a platter or a cheeseboard or even a clean wooden chopping board. Fan out the bhakri in a semicircle.

It doesn't matter how you serve – you could play catch with the packet of bhakri; won't affect the sensational taste.

Grilled Haloumi
For 6

I first ate haloumi at a Lebanese restaurant in London – crusty slices of milky, smoky, salty and slightly chewy cheese, which I could eat every day. When I discovered it was available at our local market, I was hugely smug about an opportunity to show off to gullible dinner guests.

Haloumi – 2 packets/200 gms each
Oil – a few drops to slick the pan
Mint leaves, freshly chopped – 1 tbsp

Put a heavy-based pan on the stove, and swirl a few drops of oil in it.

Thinly slice the haloumi to about the thickness of a five-rupee coin.

Once the pan is hot, place the slices on it, and give it about a minute on each side.

Serve with a garnish of chopped mint for exotic appeal.

Fresh Figs and Gorgonzola

For 6

This is the jewel of my cheese platter; perhaps because I learnt it from my friend, Neel, the most flamboyant cook I know. I envy his style, his ideas, his articulation on food and his generosity. Every single meal that he's cooked for me has been memorable. Even if he's pouring milk into my bowl of cereal, there's such style and confidence. He did the figs and Gorgonzola on the first day I ever met him – I felt very posh buying the Gorgonzola from Dean and DeLuca in New York. I think he asked for Californian figs. All very new and exotic for me.

In India, I just buy nice, dark, firm figs. The grainy, gangreny Gorgonzola against the purple figs makes it very showy.

Fresh, ripe, firm figs – 6
Red wine – 2 wine glasses
Honey – 2 tbsp
Black pepper, cracked – 1 tbsp
Thyme – 4 sprigs
Gorgonzola – 200 gms

Place the figs with their stems in a pan and press them gently to crack them slightly open.

Pour in the wine and honey and place the pan on low heat. Put in the pepper and thyme and cook on low heat as the wine reduces and gets jammy. Turn the figs every now and then so that they are evenly coated.

When the liquid is no longer runny and just about coating the fruit, take the figs out, place them on a plate and pour the remains of the pan over them.

Serve with the Gorgonzola.

Brie and Honey on Melba Toast

For 6

This is pretty common at upscale cocktails. Very easy to make – just go and buy a packet of Brie cheese.

Brie - *1 packet/250 gms*
Melba toasts – *18*
Honey, to drizzle on the cheese - *4 tbsp*
Pine nuts - *18*

Set the oven on grill. Place chunks of Brie on the melba toasts (pg 7) and top off with a squiggle of honey and the pine nuts.

Place these on a baking tray and grill for 8-10 minutes or till the Brie melts and loses its form.

Serve immediately.

Very delish, very posh.

Steamed Shrimp

For 4

This is Zen food – easy, super trendy and healthy. The catch is to get really fresh prawns. I use medium-sized prawns. It works well with shrimps too, but really big prawns are wasted on this dish

Prawns, medium-sized, shelled – 500 gms
Ginger, grated – 1-inch piece
Japanese soy sauce – ½ cup

De-vein and wash the prawns in many changes of water. Some people get rid of the tail – I could never do that.

Bring 500 ml of water to a boil in a pan or steamer.

If you have a steamer, put the cleaned prawns in it and place it over the boiling water for 3 minutes.

If you don't have a steamer, place a strainer or a colander with the prawns a few inches above the boiling water in the pan for about 4 minutes, during which time the prawns would turn opaque. Stop right there. You don't want the prawns to cook any more than that.

In a small, beautiful bowl (remember this dish is Japanese-inspired) place the ginger and pour in the soy sauce. Put this on a platter and arrange the prawns around it.

Use fingers to dip the prawns into the sauce and eat.

Looks beautiful served on a banana leaf.

Beef and Lettuce Wraps

For 6

This is a dramatic dish, flush with flavours and textures and one of my absolute party favourites. I often serve it as part of a larger meal, but it does just as well as a solo item.

Iceberg lettuce – *1 head/12-15 leaves*
Bean sprouts – *100 gms*
Mint leaves – *2 large fistfuls*
Oil – *1 tbsp*
Spring onions, finely chopped – *2*
Garlic, finely chopped – *1 clove*
Minced beef (undercut) – *400 gms*

Sauce
Fish sauce – *¼ cup*
Lime juice – *¼ cup*
Sugar – *2 tsp*
Garlic, minced – *1 clove*
Mint leaves, chopped – *2 tbsp*
Bird chillies, finely chopped – *4*

First the vegetables: Wash the lettuce in ice-cold water, dry in a salad drier or pat it dry as well as you can. Place in a plastic bag and refrigerate.

Soak the bean sprouts in ice-cold water as well, drain, dry and refrigerate.

Wash the mint leaves and refrigerate.

The idea is to have crisp, cold crunchy vegetables to offset the hot, sweet and tangy beef.

Put the oil in a pan on moderate heat. Add the spring onions and the garlic and fry till they brown. Remove with a slotted spoon.

Raise the heat and add the beef mince. Cook it for at the most a minute, turning it around to get rid of the raw pinkness. The moment it changes colour, remove from heat.

To the beef, add the fried spring onion, garlic and all the sauce ingredients.

To serve

On a large platter (white works well, setting off the greens of the leaves and chilli-flecked beef), pile the lettuce leaves, bean sprouts and mint on one side and the dressed beef mince on the other.

The idea is to fill a lettuce leaf with some of the mince, mint and bean sprouts, roll it up and eat.

Most fab.

22

Show dinners

I learnt to cook because of what was called the Dinner Party. It brought out my prime character attributes – the desire to play to an audience, to perform, to please, to sneak into people's hearts. These reasons still hold when I call people for dinner – first understated showing off, followed by acknowledgement of adulation, ending with mental backslapping.

While age has not dampened my appetite for attention, it may have given me some wisdom. No longer do I believe in the strength of numbers. Instead, I like the spectacle of one attention-grabbing main course, supported by a salad or a side dish. There's always plain white rice, or appropriate bread or noodles, depending on which dish is playing lead. Guests these days seem to enjoy the surprise of the menu and like to eat in big, hearty amounts rather than pick at too many small, nondescript and common dishes.

Khowswey

For 6, on a conservative estimate – this dish is given to overeating

Khowswey epitomises the chapter. This is my style of cooking – if there is such a thing. A one-dish dinner with little effort and immense wow factor. The steaming hot curry over the pale noodles and the bowls of multicoloured garnish, assembled by each individual, makes for one of my hottest dinners.

Chicken, skinned and cut – 1 kg
Gram flour – 1 tsp
Thin coconut milk (see note) – 3 cups
Egg noodles – 2 packets/250 gms each

Marinade
Garlic paste – 3 tsp
Ginger paste – 1 tsp
Oil – 3 tbsp
Chilli powder – 1 tsp or more
Turmeric powder – 1 tsp
Fish sauce – 2 tbsp
Salt – 2 tsp

Toppings
Garlic, finely sliced, deep fried – 12 cloves
Coriander leaves, picked and chopped – 1 cup
Spring onions, finely chopped (optional) – 1 cup
Hard-boiled eggs, diced – 6
Chilli powder – 3 tbsp
Limes, quartered – 4
Potato straws (commercial) – 200 gms

A note about the coconut milk:
My coconut milk comes straight out of a tetrapak. I pour the contents of the carton into a bowl, fill the carton with water, give it a good shake and pour into the bowl. I like a thinner consistency of the coconut milk as I think this makes the curry light, not smothered by the richness of the coconut milk.

Combine all the marinade ingredients in a bowl and marinate chicken for up to 6 hours. Aim for at least an hour.

Heat a heavy-based pan and add the chicken with all its marinade. Stir and cook till the marinade starts bubbling. Turn heat down to moderate, cover and cook for 15 minutes.

By now, the chicken would be half done and cooking in its own juices.

Stir in the gram flour and the coconut milk.

Cook on moderate heat, uncovered, for another 10-15 minutes. The chicken should be done, but not coming off the bone. This is important, as it will need to be kept warm through the dinner period.

Once the chicken cools, it's critical to taste this dish – remember it will be eaten with bland noodles, which will play off the spices from the curry. It should be well salted, spiced and giving off some heat.

To serve

Cook noodles according to instructions on the packet.

Arrange the toppings in individual bowls.

Place the noodles on a platter, the steaming chicken curry in a bowl and the smaller bowls with the garnishes on the table.

Guests should take some noodles, ladle some hot chicken curry and top off with all the garnishes.

I serve this in soup plates or bowls, as it's too runny for normal dinner plates.

Vegetarian Khowswey
For 6

Under pressure (not quite from PETA, but semi-fascist veggie friends), I caved, and did the obvious veg version, replacing the chicken with a vegetarian curry. The vegetables that taste good in this curry are those which provide a bit of a crunch, but because the dish is rich with toppings, I have settled on broccoli and tofu. Carrots, French beans, baby corn work well.

Oil – 2 tsp
Garlic paste – 2 tsp
Ginger paste – ½ tsp
Chilli powder – ½ tsp
Turmeric powder – ¼ tsp
Gram flour – 1 tsp
Coconut milk (as for the non-veg dish) – 2 cups
Salt – 1 tsp
Broccoli, cut into floretes – 1 head
Tofu, cubed – 250 gms
Noodles – 2 packets

Toppings

As for the chicken khowswey opposite

Heat the oil in a pan on moderate heat, add garlic and ginger and sauté for 2 minutes.

Sprinkle in the spice powders and cook for a minute.

Stir in the gram flour, followed by coconut milk and salt and bring to a gentle simmer.

Add the broccoli, cover pan and cook for 5 minutes.

Open the pan, add tofu, give it one last boil and switch off.

This is blander than the chicken khowswey and has a gentler, satvik appeal.

Serve it in the same way as the chicken khowswey.

Naga-Style Pork Raja Mirchi + Soupy Greens

For 6

The first time I had Naga-style cooking was at the Naga stall at Dilli Haat in Delhi. I was blown, not just by the novelty of the Naga thali, but because of the heat the raja mirchi used in this dish generated. There was sweat and tears and the kind of pleasure only a masochist understands. A stainless steel thali is served with plump boiled rice, a bowl of radiation-orange curried pork and another bowl of soothing boiled greens with its cooking liquid. After ingesting only the first morsel of the rice and curry the mouth feels paralysed, but the brain, in some kind of automated suicide mission, can't stop the hand to mouth motion of dipping spoon in curry mixed with rice and raising it to the numb and open mouth.

If you're turned off by the description, don't be. Raja mirchi, one of the hottest chillies in the world, is found only in Nagaland. While I am a raja mirchi fanatic, for my friends, I have toned it down and used Kashmiri and normal red chillies. This dish is perfect for a wintry or rainy day. The red heat of the meat, the bland white rice and the cool shades of greens floating in their bathwater make a rather enticing picture.

Pork Raja Mirchi

Oil – 1 tsp
Pork, not too bony, with at least 25 per cent fat, cut into 1-inch cubes – 1 kg
Raja mirchi – 1 or dried red chillies – 3
Dried red Kashmiri chillies – 4
Garlic – 8 cloves
Ginger – ½ inch
Salt – 1 tsp

Heat the oil in a large, heavy-based pan that has a tight-fitting lid. Once the oil warms up, add the pork and stir on high heat for a minute till all the meat loses it pinkness.

Add the chillies, garlic and ginger, but don't stir this too much. The idea is to lightly cook these in the pork juices, before extricating them from the pan to make a paste. Cover the pan.

After 10 minutes, fish out the chillies and the garlic, ideally with tongs. Place these either in a blender jar or in a mortar, along with the salt. Pulse grind coarsely.

Uncover the pan and stir the chilli-garlic paste into the cooking meat till all the meat is coated.

Cover the pan, turn heat down to moderate and cook for about 25 minutes, stirring every 7-8 minutes.

This shouldn't have gravy – the chillies should darken with the cooking. If you want a bit of gravy, add a cup of warm water and cook for 5 more minutes. This makes it fluid and easier to eat with rice.

I often use more than one lethal raja mirchi for this as an occasional endurance test for the guests.

Soupy greens

Salt – 1 tsp
Beans, any, trimmed – 6
Cabbage, roughly torn – 6 leaves
Bok choi, roughly torn – 6 leaves

Put a large pan with 2 litres of water and salt on high heat to boil.

Once the water is bubbling, put in the beans, followed by the cabbage and bok choi. Leave for 30 seconds and turn off the heat immediately.

Cover and set aside.

This is excellent diet food – I often have it as dinner during the week.

The vegetables should be eaten/slurped out of soup plates. Ladle in some rice and the vegetables with the cooking liquid. Add the meat.

show dinners

Chicken Curry 101

For 4

The idea for this book germinated from this dish. My friend Anjolie Singh – at that time a single, hotshot lawyer in London – used to go out to eat and drink every evening. Once, sitting in her posh London apartment staring at her spotlessly shiny, unused kitchen, she got an urge to entertain at home. She emailed, asking me for easy and impressive recipes. I worked out this chicken curry for her. I believe some of her friends, who know a thing or two about cooking and eating, asked for the recipe

About a year later, I was visiting my friend Yahel Chirinian's family in Avignon. Yahel's Maman Elizabeth is a relentless Jewish mother – she thinks nothing of cooking gigantic Provençal meals full of fresh vegetables, meats and cheeses, and desserts like baba au rhum (swimming in rum) for her daughter's middle-aged friends. One day, after copious consumption of Elizabeth's hospitality, I offered to cook. I chose my own chicken recipe (till then untested). This turned out one of the best chicken curries I have ever eaten. Perhaps it was the free-range chicken, which I bought for 20 euros, that made the difference. There is something to be said about first-rate, farm-fresh ingredients.

Chicken, skinned and cut – 1 kg
Oil, mustard or olive – 1 tbsp
Bay leaves – 2
Coriander powder – 1 tsp

Marinade
Garlic paste – 3 heaped tbsp
Ginger paste – 1 tsp
Salt – 1 tsp
Chilli powder – ½-1 tsp or more if you can stomach hot; I use two
Turmeric powder – ½ tsp
Bay leaves, crushed – 2
Oil, mustard or olive – 1 tbsp

Combine the marinade ingredients in a bowl. Mix in the chicken and marinate it for 2-6 hours in the refrigerator. I often do this in the morning before I go to work.

Heat the oil in a deep pan and add the bay leaves followed by the chicken with its marinade.

Give this a good stir, turn down the heat to moderate, sprinkle in the coriander powder, cover and simmer for 25 minutes.

Heat a cup of water in a kettle. Take off the lid. The chicken should be cooked by now, and an angry reddish brown colour.

Add the hot water and boil it down a bit. This dish should be runny.

To be eaten with basmati rice and a kachumbar salad.

Variation

For a kg of chicken, use 3 medium-sized potatoes. Peel and halve lengthwise. Heat 3 tbsp of oil (mustard is distinctive) in a frying pan, brown the potatoes and take out on paper towels. When the curry has been cooking for 15 minutes, open the pan, add the potatoes, stir it along with the rest of the ingredients, add the cup of hot water and cover. It should be done in 15 minutes. In this version, you need to increase the salt – ½ tsp for 3 potatoes.

Kachumbar (Minced Onion, Tomato and Cucumber Salad)
For 6

This is more a relish than a real salad.

Onion, medium-sized, finely chopped – 1
Tomato, medium-sized, finely chopped – 1
Capsicum, medium-sized, finely chopped – ½
Cucumber, finely chopped – 1
Green chilli, finely chopped – 1
Coriander and/or mint leaves, chopped (optional) – 1 tbsp
Mustard , Coleman's English or kashundi (available in some supermarkets in the metros) – to taste
Garlic paste – ½ tsp
Olive oil – 1 tbsp
Sugar – ½ tsp

Put the vegetables in a bowl and give them a toss.

Mix the mustard, garlic paste, olive oil and the sugar. Pour it over the salad just before eating, after tossing everything around for a bit.

Chicken Tea Soup

For 6

This is a marvellous dish – as easy as making a cup of tea. Its appeal lies in its simplicity and the explosion of flavours that follows with almost no effort at all.

Garlic – 1 whole head
Onion, large – 1
Lemon grass – 2 plump stalks
Chicken, whole, with skin – 800 gms to 1 kg
Ginger or galangal – 2-inch piece
Kaffir lime leaves – 10-12
Salt – 2 tsp
Coconut milk at room temperature, straight from a tetrapak – 200 ml
Bird chillies, chopped – 3
Egg noodles, cooked (optional) – 100 gms

Take the entire garlic bulb and cut it into half along the equator. Do the same with the onion. Trim off the dry bits of the lemon grass, and smash the fat root with a blunt instrument.

Put 3 litres of water in a pressure cooker. Add the garlic, onion, lemon grass, the whole chicken, ginger or galangal, lime leaves and salt.

Cook under pressure for 40-50 minutes on low heat after the cooker reaches full pressure. Remove from heat and let it cool naturally till the pressure subsides.

Just as you would for tea, strain the contents of the cooker by pouring it into a colander placed over a deep bowl. Keep the chicken aside and discard everything else in the colander.

Quickly skin the chicken, and shred about one-third of it. Save the rest for some other purpose.

In individual soup bowls, put about 1 tbsp or more of shredded chicken and pour in a portion of the soup.

Add the coconut milk according to preference, like you would for tea. (Make sure the coconut milk is at room temperature, to avoid curdling.)

Top off each bowl with ½ tsp of chopped bird chillies, which bleed into the heavenly whiteness of the hot and lemony soup.

To add a bit more substance and make a meal of this soup, put some cooked rice noodles into the bowls along with the chicken. The noodles get cooked when the hot soup is poured in.

Cold Noodles with Vegetables and/or
Chicken in a Sesame Sauce

For 4

This is a very stylish meal – I often serve small portions of it when I have people over for drinks. It makes for an excellent packed lunch or picnic food. You can vary the ingredients. Often, I don't use noodles at all. The only rule for this dish is that it should be served cold, like revenge.

Carrot, cut into matchsticks – 1
Celery, diced – 1 stalk
Chicken, cut into pieces (optional) – 400 gms
Salt – ½ tsp + 1 tsp
Noodles – 300 gms
Cucumber, chopped in small chunks – 1

Sauce
Tahini/sesame paste – 1 tbsp
Peanut butter – 1 tsp
Lime juice – 2 tbsp
Soy sauce – 4 tbsp
Sugar – 1 tbsp
Sesame oil – 1 tbsp
Salt – a pinch

Boil the carrots and celery in water with ½ tsp salt for about 3 minutes. Drain and refrigerate.

If using chicken, put the pieces in a pan, cover with water and salt and cook till the pieces become opaque. Drain, reserve the liquid and refrigerate the chicken.

Boil the noodles – normal egg noodles or udon are good – in water with 1 tsp salt. Drain and cool.

The critical part of this is the sauce. I like it thin with just a hint of the flavours, as it has two heavy ingredients, namely the tahini and the peanut butter. Mix all the ingredients for the sauce and beat it to make a sauce – about as thin as double cream.

When it's time to serve, mix the runny sauce into the noodles till each strand of noodle is coated. Add the crunchy veggies, the cucumber and the chicken (if used).

This stays well. If you're not going to eat it soon, leave it in the refrigerator, but it's better to eat it while the veggies are still crunchy.

Wintry Sausage and Mustard Pasta

For 4

This is quite a posh meal on a winter evening, with a glass of robust red wine, perhaps a rocket salad and a warm dessert like a chocolate mud pie and ice cream (with candied orange peel, of course, page 134). For serious eaters, not fussy dieters.

Small pasta, orechiette, penne at a crunch – 200 gms
Salt – 1 tbsp
Olive oil – 1 tbsp
Garlic, minced – 1 clove
Fresh basil leaves – 100 gms
Sausage, chorizo, other Italian sausages or masala sausage – 400 gms
Mustard, Coleman's or kashundi or a blend – 1 tbsp
Cream – 200 ml
Chilli flakes – to taste

Put the pasta to boil in 1 litre of water and salt.

Heat the oil in a pan, add garlic and half the basil, stir-fry till the garlic changes colour and the basil turns crunchy. Take it out with a slotted spoon.

Chop the sausages coarsely so that some of the meat is out of the casing and some within. (A lot of people I know just use the sausage meat, but I like to bite into a bit of tightly-packed sausage too.)

In the same pan used for the garlic and basil, put in the chopped sausage and let it cook on moderate-low heat, giving out juices, for about 4 minutes.

Stir in the remaining basil, the mustard and the cream. Stir and cook on very low heat till it is bubbling. Turn off the heat.

Drain the pasta, saving 1-2 cups of the boiling water.

Add pasta to the sauce. Blend in some of the pasta water to thin out the sauce.

Spoon into individual bowls or plates. Top off with some of the fried garlic and basil, and some chilli flakes.

Rocket and Parmesan Salad

For 4

Rocket leaves – *200 gms*
The best olive oil – *2 tbsp*
Parmesan – *8 shavings (with a vegetable peeler)*

Wash the salad and spin it dry in a salad spinner. (I endorse this gizmo big time. Crunchy greens are the key to fresh, crisp salad. Costs nothing.) Or pat dry with paper towels. If you do this in advance, keep the rocket in the refrigerator.

When you're about to eat (the pasta is bubbling away, the room is filled with the aroma of the sausages and basil and the guests can't wait for their windfall), take out the rocket from the refrigerator and pour the olive oil over it.

You could either serve the salad with Parmesan shavings on top or grate it over the salad.

Pasta with Basil and Tomato + My House Salad

Pasta with Basil and Tomato

For 4

The basis of this recipe is the *River Café Cookbook*. I have just tweaked the amounts a bit. Hearty, honest and a sure-shot hit.

Tomatoes – 500 gms
Garlic – 4 cloves
Dried red chillies – 6
Extra virgin olive oil (it makes a difference in this recipe) – 2 tbsp
Fresh basil leaves – 50 gms/2 handfuls
Salt – ½ tsp + 1 tbsp
Sugar (optional) – a pinch
Pasta, penne or fusili – 400 gms

Topping

Parmesan, grated – to taste
Black pepper, freshly ground – to taste

With a sharp knife, score the tomatoes, put them in a large bowl and pour boiling water over them. Keep them submerged for a minute, take them out with a slotted spoon and plunge them into iced water. Once the torture therapy is over, drain the water, peel the skins off and chop the tomato flesh coarsely.

Peel the garlic and cut each clove into half, lengthwise.

Tear the chillies into small bits.

Heat the oil in a pan on moderate heat.

Add the garlic and chillies to the hot oil, wait for them to brown and remove with a slotted spoon.

Put the basil into the pan, and stir till it turns crunchy and infuses the oil with its flavour. Remove from the pan and save.

Add the chopped tomatoes to the oil. Cook gently for 10-12 minutes, till they turn mushy.

Add ½ tsp of salt. Sometimes, if the tomatoes are too sour, a pinch of sugar is recommended.

Cook the pasta in plenty of boiling water with 1 tbsp of salt till just done. Pasta should never be too soft – it should be hard enough to bite, or al dente. Drain and set aside.

Mix the tomato sauce into the pasta. Stir in the garlic, chillies and basil.

Spoon into individual plates or bowls.

Grate Parmesan and freshly milled pepper on top. Serve with my house salad.

My House Salad

For 4

Dressing
Olive oil – 4 tbsp
Honey – 1 tsp
Mustard – 1 tsp
Garlic, crushed – 1 clove
Thyme, fresh – 3-4 sprigs
Lime juice – 1 tbsp
Red wine vinegar – 1 tbsp

Salad
Salad greens/lettuce – 300 gms
Red bell pepper – 1
Yellow bell pepper – 1
Avocado – 1
Onion, small, sliced into rings – 1
Black olives – 2 tbsp
Walnut, pine nut or sunflower seeds, roasted – 2 tbsp

The quickest way to make the dressing is to put all the ingredients in a jar with a tight lid and shake it up without mercy. For all those who think cooking is a stress buster, this is the pinnacle of catharsis.

Tear the lettuce leaves, wash them well and dry them in a salad spinner. (You have to get this if you don't have it. Available very cheap and locally.) Keep it in the refrigerator.

Wash and chop the peppers the size of croutons.

Minutes before serving, dice the avocado.

Combine all the salad ingredients in a nice bowl (salads have to be served in something interesting – some artists who called me for dinner used an earthen pot lined with banana leaves).

Pour the dressing on top. Toss and serve.

Penne with Pumpkin, Onion, Basil and Pine Nuts

For 4

My friend Tara cooked this for me in London. She used the most deliciously smooth butternut squash. It works just as well with our pumpkin – the humble kaddu.

Extra virgin olive oil – *2 tbsp*
Red pumpkin, cubed – *250 gms*
Onions, large, cubed – *2*
Sea salt – *½ tsp*
Black pepper, freshly ground – *to taste*
Basil – *2 fistfuls*
Salt – *1 tbsp*
Penne – *350 gms*
Cream – *¾ cup*
Parmesan, grated – *for topping*
Pine nuts, toasted – *2 tbsp*
Rocket leaves (optional) – *a handful*

Set the oven at 180°C.

Pour a generous glug of extra virgin into an ovenproof dish, swirl it around so that it covers the base and sides of the dish.

Spread the cubed pumpkin and onions in the dish. Pour some more olive oil and sprinkle sea salt and pepper.

Cover the dish and place in the oven for about 30 minutes. Check every 10 minutes or so and turn the veggies around, basting them with some of the olive oil and the juices.

After checking once, tear a few of the basil leaves and throw them into the dish.

Boil plenty of water with salt and cook the pasta till just done. Reserve ½ a cup of the cooking liquid.

Mix the vegetables with the pasta in a serving dish. Pour in the cream and some of the cooking liquid to blend it nicely.

Grate some Parmesan, grind some pepper and sprinkle the pine nuts and remaining basil leaves on top.

Some chopped rocket leaves add that complex flavour. Add it when you're assembling the dish.

Very fresh, healthy flavours.

Easy Pork Vindaloo

For 6

This dish has gone through so many stages that it's almost lost its vindaloo identity. Call it Vindaloo-inspired pork curry.

Pork, with 25 per cent fat, cubed – *1 kg*
Oil – *1 tbsp*
Onion, medium-sized, sliced – *1*
Curry leaves – *2 sprigs*
Salt – *½ tsp*

Spice paste
Dried red chillies – *4*
Dried Kashmiri red chillies – *6*
Garlic – *10 cloves*
Cumin seeds – *1 tsp*
Mustard seeds – *1 tsp*
Cloves – *4 tsp*
White vinegar – *4 tbsp*

Combine all the ingredients for the spice paste and set aside for an hour or so. Grind into a smooth paste.

If you have time, marinate the pork in the spice paste. If not…

Heat the oil in a heavy-based pan or even a pressure cooker. Put in the onion and cook for 2 minutes, till translucent.

Add the pork, the spice paste, curry leaves and salt (or the marinated meat if you had soaked it) and cook on high heat till it starts boiling.

Turn the heat down, cover and cook for 40-45 minutes in a normal pan, or 20 minutes in the pressure cooker after it has reached full pressure.

This is a hot dish, great with crusty bread and cool kachumbar (page 29). Rice is good too.

Cheese and Spinach Pork with Red Chillies (aka Recipe for Disaster*)

For 6-8

This is one of those recipes we are forbidden from sharing. It came into my life through Lalidi – my non-biological sister. She's a fat girl in a thin girl's body. Her super power is cheese pork! She learnt this from her Bhutanese friends in school in Kalimpong. Those of us who have eaten this, have been her mental slaves ever since.

*The dish is so rich that one day's pleasure equals a complete hole in any kind of diet.

Dried Kashmiri red chillies – 6
Dried red chillies – 6
Boneless pork, with at least 30 per cent fat, cubed – 1 kg
Spinach – 500 gms
Oil – 1 tbsp
Processed cheese, Amul or equivalent, or Cheddar, grated – 250-400 gms (some like more!)
Salt – to taste

Soak the chillies in a cup of warm water for about an hour. If you're in a hurry (my speciality), cook the soaked chillies on high in the microwave for a minute, or gently simmer them while preparing the rest of the ingredients.

Wash the pork and set aside to drain.

Wash the spinach thoroughly in several changes of water and chop it. No shortcuts here.

Put a pressure cooker or a heavy-based pan with the oil to heat.

When the oil is hot, add the pork, and quickly stir it to get rid of the rawness – 20 seconds if you've been working out.

Put in the spinach. Suddenly you'll feel the pot is crowded and there's no space to manoeuvre. Just let it be for a minute. Spinach wilts in no time. Before you know, it would have reduced considerably.

Add the chillies with the soaking water and the cheese. Stir this bubbling pot and mix everything.

If you're using the pressure cooker, close it and cook under pressure on low heat for about 20 minutes after the cooker reaches full pressure. If not, cover the pan and cook for around 35-40 minutes.

Almost immediately after you take the pressure cooker off, hold the cooker under a gentle stream of tap water away from your face till the hissing subsides. This is an indication that the pressure is off.

Put the cooker back on heat and gently open it. Cook on moderate heat for about 10 minutes, till the water from the spinach evaporates, making this into a gooey mass with the most spectacular visual effect.

If you're not using pressure, open the pan and cook till the water evaporates.

I usually omit the salt, as the cheese is salty enough. If you need to add some, do so.

This is best with plump rice. Can be an excellent picnic meal too, with bread.

Gado Gado

For 6

For the sins of the previous recipe, I give you Gado Gado – fresh, wholesome, nourishing, delicious, spectacular Indonesian magic meal in a salad. You can serve this in small bowls as a starter or as the main dish. It's a medley of veggies, the crunchiest of them being bean sprouts, with a divinely silky peanut dressing.

Dressing
Peanuts, roasted – 1 cup
Oil – 2 tsp
Garlic, finely chopped – 2 cloves
Shallots, finely chopped – 2 or onion, finely chopped – ½
Salt – ½ tsp
Chilli powder – ½ tsp
Brown sugar or jaggery – 1 tsp
Lime juice – 2 tbsp or more
Black pepper, freshly ground – 1 heaped tsp or more

Salad
French beans – 250 gms
Carrot – 1
Broccoli or cauliflower, medium-sized – 1 head
Cabbage – 1/3
Bean sprouts – 250 gms
Salt – 1 tsp
Cucumber, medium-sized – 1
Potato, large, hard-boiled – 1
Eggs, less than hard-boiled – 2

Dressing

Grind the peanuts in a blender. I stop before it's totally powdery.

Heat the oil in a pan and add the garlic and shallots or onions. Sauté till they are light brown.

Add a cup of warm water, powdered peanuts, salt, chilli powder and brown sugar or jaggery and stir to ensure there are no objectionable lumps.

Turn off the heat. Add lime juice and pepper. Taste. This is not as simple as it sounds – it's too sweet at first, so you add some lime, then tart, so you add some pepper. The trick is to taste a bit and wait for all the flavours to settle down before taking a call.

Salad

The idea is to have all the vegetables slightly crunchy but short of raw. So depending on cooking time this is what I do:

The beans should be strung and trimmed, and cut into 2-3 pieces. The carrot should be cut into sticks about the same size.

Broccoli or cauliflower should be just the flowers – get rid of the hard stems. (Save them for a soup or throw into mixed vegetables with garlic and fish sauce.)

The cabbage should be shredded long (prettier) and the bean sprout tailed and trimmed a bit.

Now, put a large, deep pan on high heat with about 3 litres of water and the salt.

Once the water is on a roiling boil, start adding the raw vegetables starting from the hardest: carrots and beans first, and after a minute the broccoli or cauliflower, followed by cabbage and bean sprouts. Turn the heat off immediately and drain everything dry in a colander. Leave it to drip some more in the colander, in the refrigerator.

Slice the cucumbers, not too fine though. Cut the boiled potatoes to the size of the carrots and the eggs in eighths.

To serve

Purists serve everything in separate dishes. My guests are lazy and clumsy, so I like to serve all the vegetables in one big platter and the dressing separately.

Arrange the vegetables and eggs on a platter either in colour-coordinated separate rows or mixed together. It's important it's all mixed up well so that you're not accused of bias in the portions. I could easily avoid the carrots, and take double helpings of the potatoes and eggs!

Pour the dressing on top generously or serve it alongside.

Garlic Kadhi + Masala Bhindi

Garlic Kadhi

For 4

I saw this recipe in some old magazine. Wilting under comparison with my mother-in-law, Swati Patel's (she is an extraordinary cook) stratospheric Gujarati kadhi, I decided to douse mine in garlic. It's one of my favourites.

Yogurt – 3 heaped tbsp
Gram flour – 1 tbsp
Oil or ghee – 1 tsp + 1 tbsp
Mustard seeds – ¼ tsp
Cumin seeds – ½ tsp
Fenugreek seeds – ¼ tsp
Asafoetida powder – ¼ tsp
Turmeric powder – ¼ tsp
Salt – 1 tsp
Garlic paste – 1 tsp
Garlic, chopped – 3 cloves

Beat the yogurt with the gram flour into a smooth paste. Add 2½ cups of water. This is my method; it eliminates lumps in the kadhi, which are formed if gram flour is mixed into diluted yogurt.

Heat a kadhai and add 1 tsp oil or ghee. When hot, turn down the heat and add mustard, cumin, fenugreek and asafoetida, stir to mix and let the seeds splutter. Pour in the watered-down yogurt.

Once it comes to a boil, add the turmeric, salt and the garlic paste, turn down the heat and cook for 5 minutes, pretty much stirring the kadhi all the time.

Simultaneously, in another small pan, heat 1 tbsp oil or ghee. (I recommend ½ tbsp oil and ½ tbsp ghee).

When hot, plunge in the chopped garlic. In a minute, this will start turning colour. Either you could pour the entire contents of the pan into the boiling kadhi, cook for a minute and turn off; or in a quick action, which involves a slotted spoon, take the garlic out and transfer it into the kadhi.

Either way, a guilt-free mood lifter.

show dinners

Masala Bhindi (Spiced Okra)

For 4

The success of this depends entirely on the ingredients – my mother-in-law insists on getting me the best dhana-jeeru (coriander-cumin) powder from our Patel relatives who grind their own spices in Katargam, near Surat. It makes a difference not just in taste, but in the texture – home-made spices have a rougher texture – which I find reassuring. For this dish, it would be worth the effort to take whole coriander and cumin, roast in a dry pan for 2 minutes and grind it coarsely in a grinder.

Okra, trimmed – 16
Oil – 1 tbsp
Fenugreek seeds – ½ tsp
Asafoetida powder – ¼ tsp
Salt – ½ tsp
Chilli powder – ½ tsp or more if you like heat
Turmeric powder – ½ tsp
Coriander powder, home-made – 3 tbsp; commercial – 2 tbsp
Cumin powder, home-made – 3 tbsp; commercial – 2 tbsp
Gram flour (optional) – 1 tsp

Cut the okra evenly; an average okra into 3 pieces.

Heat the oil in a pan on moderate heat. Add the fenugreek and asafoetida and swiftly add the okra, followed after a minute by the salt and spice powders. Stir and cook on high heat for a minute. Turn down the heat and cook till done, for about 15 minutes.

As a finishing touch, sprinkle the gram flour over the vegetable before you turn the heat off. It serves the same purpose as a touch-up to your make-up; gets rid of the oily look.

Sunday Mutton Curry with Potatoes

For 6, with some left over

For many meat-eating Indians, Sunday lunch is the mutton curry day. In the lanes of Kolkata where I grew up, the sound of pressure cooker whistles followed by the wafting aroma of mutton curry were the sounds and smells of comfort. One of my male colleagues takes pride in the fact that he cooks only on Sundays, making mutton curry, not because he wants to give his wife a break from daily cooking, but only because he's worried hers won't be as special as his.

While my mother thinks this mutton curry is too homely to be served when we're having company, guests universally love it. Because it's a thin curry, I recommend using a pressure cooker – no virtue in not using one. It's the runny curry, the chewy bones and the soft potatoes that make it so hot.

Mutton pieces – 1 kg
Mustard oil – 4 tbsp
Onions, medium-sized, cut in chunks – 2
Potatoes, medium-sized – 4
Bay leaves – 2
Cumin seeds – 1 tsp

Marinade
Garlic paste – 4 tsp
Ginger paste – 1½ tsp
Chilli powder – at least ½ tsp, up to 3 for ultra heat
Turmeric powder – ½ tsp
Coriander powder – 1 tsp
Mustard oil – 2 tbsp

Combine the marinade ingredients and rub it into the mutton. It's always good to marinate for at least an hour. I just keep it as long as it takes me to get everything else ready.

Put the oil to heat in the pressure cooker. When it gets to smoking, throw in the onions and turn the heat down. Cook on moderate heat till they turn brown. Add a generous sprinkling of water while frying.

Once they start turning brown, remove on to a paper-towel bed.

Peel the potatoes and cut each into two vertically.

Increase the heat for the oil to get very hot again. Add the potatoes, flat side down, keep for a minute and turn over. Control the heat so that the potatoes don't get burnt but develop a golden crust.

Remove potatoes on to a bed of paper towels.

With a spoon, get rid of all the oil except for 1 tsp. Return the cooker to moderate heat and add the bay leaves, slightly crushed by hand, and the cumin seeds. Give this a stir. You will smell the lovely aroma in a few seconds.

Add the marinated mutton, raise the heat and stir this for 1-2 minutes, till the contents start bubbling. Cover with a non-pressure lid and cook for 15 minutes.

Rinse the bowl in which the meat was marinating with warm water (it's a smart way to use every last bit of the spices) and reserve the water.

After 15 minutes, uncover the cooker, add the potatoes and stir it into the rest of the curry. Pour in the reserved spiced water.

Close the cooker and pressure-cook on low heat for 10 minutes after the cooker reaches full pressure. Let it cool naturally.

Recommended hot, with a kachumbar salad (page 29) and a squeeze of lime for those who like it.

Fish and Chips

Only the classy can pull this off – fish and chips and cold beer! The fish should be big, white and firm, the potatoes smooth. Should start frying only when guests are ready to eat.

Fried Fish

For 4

Fillet of firm white fish like pomfret, bekti, rawas – *1 kg / 5-6 fillets*
Lime juice – *4 tbsp*
Garlic – *5 cloves*
Ginger – *1-inch piece*
Green chillies – *4*
Coriander leaves – *a bunch/1 cup*
Salt – *1 tsp*
Oil for deep-frying
Breadcrumbs – *1 cup*
Egg – *1*

Wash the fish in several changes of water. Dry with paper towels. Pour lime juice over the fillets. Stand for 30 minutes.

Make a paste of the garlic, ginger, chillies, coriander leaves and salt in a blender.

Take the fish out of its citrus soak, towel down thoroughly and anoint each of the fillets in the green paste from the blender.

Lay all the fillets in a dish, cover in cling film and refrigerate. This should be done for at least 2 hours, 4 is good.

When guests are ready to eat, put a deep frying pan with oil to heat. Spread a newspaper and make a fat bed of breadcrumbs. (A tray is good too, but why bother? Newspaper is perfect to wrap up the mess once you're done.)

Break an egg into a shallow bowl and beat it to merge the yolk and white.

Take the fish out of the refrigerator and shake off as much of the green paste as you can. Place this in the egg, lift and drop into the bed of crumbs. It's critical to keep one hand dry or else you'll have a messy, wet sandy feel. Dredge the fish through the crumbs, lift with the dry hand and turn over so that the other side gets coated.

Depending on how you like the fish – purists like as little coating as possible, I like the crust as much as I do the fish – you can choose to fry it in hot oil or repeat the egg bath and the dredging process and then fry in hot oil.

Take it out of the fat just as soon as it turns golden – by the time it comes out, it's darker by a few shades.

To be eaten with ketchup, mustard or mayo, and fries, of course.

French Fries or Finger Chips

For 4

Once you perfect them, you can have your own fan club.

Potatoes, large, kept whole – 6
Salt – 2 tbsp
Oil – 1 litre
Sea salt – to taste
Black pepper, freshly ground – to taste

Fill a deep pan with 5 litres of water. Put in the potatoes and the salt while the water is cold. Cover the pan and bring to a boil on high heat. Turn down the heat and cook the potatoes for 7-8 minutes.

Turn off the heat, take out the potatoes and place them in a bowl of cold water.

About 10 minutes before the guests are ready to eat, put a heavy-based frying pan with the oil to heat.

While the oil heats (this will take at least 5 minutes due to the quantity of the oil), peel and cut the potatoes into stubby French fries. (I like mine fat and squat.)

When the oil is smoking, dunk in a batch of fries – a batch equals enough space for every fry to float on the surface when done. Turn the heat down to moderate. The fries will bubble as you put them in; the closer they are to being ready, they will stop bubbling, as most of the moisture is out.

Keep a bed of paper towels ready. At the first signs of the chips turning golden, transfer from the frying pan on to the absorbent bed.

Make sure all the fries are out before you put in the next batch. You don't want a solitary bitter chip ruining the fresh fries.

If there is a dish that deserves a sprinkling of sea salt, this is it. And generous twists from the pepper mill.

Hot home-made fries will give you enough friendship miles and transform you to a platinum cardholder.

Chicken Stew + Rice + Papad

For 4-5

When I talk of the one-dish dinner party, I think of a hot stew, something crunchy like a papad and comforting basmati rice at the wee hours of the morning, which gives second wind to the party. I speak from experience.

While there are hundreds of stews both in the Western and Indian traditions, the one I find most showy is the Kerala stew. The heat from the pepper, the sweetness from the coconut milk and the onions and the big burst of flavours from the other spices makes this dish very posh.

Onions, large – 3
Shallots – 5 or onion, small – 1
Ginger – 2-inch piece
Potatoes, medium-sized – 2
Oil – 3 tsp + 1 tbsp
Green cardamoms – 4
Cloves – 4
Cinnamon – 2-inch stick
Whole black peppercorns – 2 tsp
Plain flour – 1 tsp
Chicken, skinned and cut – 1 kg
Coconut milk (see my note alongside the recipe for khowswey, page 24) – 1¾ cups
Salt – 1 tsp
Green chillies, slit – 6
Curry leaves – 2 sprigs

Slice the 3 large onions lengthwise, and chop the shallots or small onion.

Cut the ginger into matchsticks.

Peel and cut the potatoes like French fries. Soak them in cold water.

Heat 3 tsp of oil in a kadhai or wok. When hot, toss in the whole spices and give it a stir.

Add the sliced onions and ginger and stir and cook till the onions turn translucent. Ensure they do not brown, as this will darken the pristine white stew.

Stir in the flour (to prevent the coconut milk from curdling). This should not take more than seconds.

Add the chicken and stir on high heat.

Pour in the coconut milk.

Once the milk is in, add salt, cover and cook on moderate heat for 15 minutes.

Open the pan, add the potatoes and chillies, cover and cook for another 15 minutes.

Heat 1 tbsp of oil in a small pan. In Kerala, the oil that is most commonly used at this stage is coconut. If you don't have the stomach for it, use your normal oil.

When the oil heats up, put in the chopped shallots or onion and the curry leaves and fry till brown. Turn off the heat. With a slotted spoon, transfer the fried shallots or onion and curry leaves into the bubbling stew.

Most pleasurable hot, with rice and crisp-fried papad.

***Variation:* Vegetable Stew**
This stew is lovely with vegetables too. I use potato, carrot, beans, broccoli (1 kg in all). After frying the onions and spices and adding the flour, pour in the coconut milk. Cook the carrots (cut in long sticks), potatoes and beans with the pan covered for 15 minutes. Five minutes before adding the curry leaves and shallots/onion, add the broccoli. All the vegetables should have some bite to them and not be overcooked.

show dinners

Dark, Aromatic Chicken Curry + South Indian Raita

For 6

Dark, Aromatic Chicken Curry

This dish has the rarest combination of spices I have ever eaten – not just in Indian food. It uses pepper, coriander and fenugreek as its main spice mix, supported by cinnamon, resulting in the most aromatic, dark, magical curry.

Coriander seeds – 3 tbsp
Whole black peppercorns – 1 tbsp
Fenugreek seeds – 1 tsp
Oil – 3 tbsp
Mustard seeds – 1 tsp
Cinnamon – 3 x 1-inch sticks
Chicken, skinned and cut – 1 kg
Onions, medium-sized, sliced lengthwise – 2
Garlic, sliced – 2 cloves
Ginger, grated – ½-inch piece
Tomato, medium-sized, chopped – 1
Lime juice – 1 tsp
Coconut milk (see my note alongside the recipe for khowswey, page 24) – 1 cup
Salt – ½-1 tsp
Green chillies, slit – 2-6

Heat a small, heavy-based pan on moderate heat. I have a small cast iron kadhai, which is perfect for this step. When it heats up, sprinkle in the coriander seeds, peppercorns and fenugreek seeds. Lower the heat, stirring to prevent the spices from burning, till aromatic. Remove from heat.

Once the spices cool a bit, empty them into a blender jar and powder.

Heat oil in a large pan or a kadhai and add the mustard seeds and cinnamon.

Quickly add the chicken and stir-fry in batches, till they lose their pinkness. Remove with a slotted spoon.

In the same oil, add the onions, garlic and ginger and cook on moderate heat till the onions are soft.

Add the spices from the blender and stir-fry for 3-4 minutes.

Blend the tomatoes into this dark mixture and cook for another 2-3 minutes or till all the spices and vegetables are amalgamated and bubbles of oil emanate from this aromatic gravy. Stir in the lime juice.

Add the chicken, stir and cook for a minute, followed by the coconut milk and salt. Cover and cook on moderate heat for 30-40 minutes.

Open the lid, add the green chillies and turn off the heat.

To be eaten with basmati rice and South Indian Raita.

South Indian Raita
For 6

All raitas are cool and delicious – this comes with a twist. It has a hint of sugar, the sharpness of mustard and the bitterness of curry leaves. Absolutely glorious with hot and complex dishes like the one above.

Sugar – 1 tsp
Mustard, English or Bengali kashundi – 1 tbsp
Yogurt – 400 gms
Fresh coconut, grated – ½ cup
Cucumber, medium-sized, grated – 1
Oil – 1 tsp
Mustard seeds – 1 tsp
Dried red chillies – 2
Curry leaves – 2 sprigs

Whisk the sugar and mustard into the yogurt. Mix in the coconut and cucumber. Pour into a serving bowl.

Refrigerate, covered in cling film.

Just before serving, heat the oil in a small pan. Add the mustard seeds followed by the dried red chillies and the curry leaves.

When the chillies change colour, pour the contents of the pan over the yogurt mix. Do not stir it in.

Prawn Balchao + Garlic Pao + Cucumber Salad

Prawn Balchao
For 6

This is a fun take on the Goan balchao. It is what I make sometimes for guests who come by for drinks but the conversation and the mood turn so addictive, that I force them to stay for dinner. It may be easy and last-minute, but tastes sensational, overloaded with spices, chillies and vinegar, doused by the cool of the cucumber salad. I use shrimps or medium-sized prawns. Don't waste your big prawns on this.

Shelled prawns or shrimps – 500 gms
Oil – 2 tbsp
Cumin seeds – 1 tbsp
Curry leaves – 12
Onions, large, minced – 2
Garlic paste – 1 heaped tsp
Ginger paste – ½ tsp
Coriander powder, coarsely ground preferable – 1 tbsp
Chilli powder – ½ tsp
Salt – ½-1 tsp
White or malt vinegar – ½ cup

De-vein and wash the prawns and leave them in a colander to drain.

Heat the oil in a pan on moderate heat. Add the cumin seeds and curry leaves, followed by the onions in 30 seconds.

Stir and cook for a couple of minutes.

Add the garlic and ginger, lower the heat to moderate and cook unhurriedly for another 2-3 minutes.

Add the spice powders and stir and cook. If this starts to stick to the pan, splash in some water. Cook for a few more minutes till the oil starts bubbling out of the mixture.

Raise the heat, add the prawns, stir them in quickly and fry for 2 minutes.

Add salt and vinegar, cover the pan and cook for 1-2 minutes, till the surface of the dish resembles a reddish oil slick.

This can be eaten cold, most conducive for parties that show no signs of ending.

Garlic Pao

For 6

In Mumbai, Goa Portuguesa serves the best garlic pao. The owner, Mitr Suhas Awchat, takes up a lot of my eating time there talking about the difference between pao and pav, which I don't pay any heed to, lulled by the real thing. But he deserves credit for the perfectly chargrilled (he says the restaurant uses a wood-fired oven), crusty chunks of butter-garlic-carb heaven. My recipe is only an approximation. You need a real fire for that deliciously charred taste.

Garlic – 15 cloves
Butter – 2 tbsp/50 gms
Pao – 10

Set the grill on at 180°C.

Make a rough paste with the garlic and mix in the butter.

Slit the pao.

Once the grill is hot, place pao on a baking tray, soft side up for about 5 minutes, or till a crust forms. Take them out.

Once the pao have cooled enough to handle, butter generously and close the pao. Put them back under the grill for another 5 minutes.

For me, this could be a one-course dinner. I dream of the stuff.

Cucumber Salad

For 6

Cucumber, medium-sized, diced – 1
Spring onions, bulb only, diced – 3
Red bird chilli, minced – 1

Dressing
Sugar – ½ tsp
Salt – a pinch
White or malt vinegar – 1 tsp
Olive oil – 1 tbsp

Mix the cucumber, spring onions and bird chilli in a bowl.

Whisk the dressing ingredients in a small bowl.

Just before eating, pour the dressing over the vegetables.

This is better when cold.

Steak in Minutes + Rocket and Tomato Salad + Mashed Potatoes

Steak in Minutes

For 6

I'm too snooty to follow trends, but one that I like from our times is the snobbery about ingredients. I love the trend in the West where it's all about fresh, seasonal produce. In India, we take this for granted. A year in our family journeys from the season's first jackfruit, to mango, to lychee, to hilsa, to papdi (small flat beans peculiar to southern Gujarat), to ponk (indescribably glorious – a spongy green grain of a kind of millet). To take the grains out, the sheaf is smoked and beaten. Ponk is a speciality of Surat. It's eaten with hot and sweet green chutney, peppery sev and white sugar-coated fennel seeds. For me, ponk, which is available for less than a month between mid-December and January, is the pinnacle of Gujarati snacks – hot, sweet, salty, textured.

I digress. The point I'm trying to make is, we've come a long way from unrecognisably sludgy dishes doused in white sauce that went as 'baked dishes' during a certain period of our gastronomic history.

The beauty of this recipe is its simplicity – it's my husband Aakar's speciality. The trick is to buy fresh undercut.

Beef, undercut – *1 kg*
Olive oil – *½ cup*
Garlic, roughly chopped – *12 cloves*
Mustard, any strong, including wasabi – *4 tbsp*
Whole black peppercorns – *12*

Cut the undercut into medallions – as thick as a hamburger patty.

Whisk all the remaining ingredients in a bowl and marinate the medallions in this for at least 6 hours in the refrigerator, turning it over every hour or so. (This is beef. This is not a recipe if you're in a hurry. You wouldn't want to spoil the effect by rushing.)

If you have a heavy cast iron grill pan, this is the time to use it. If not, use something heavy.

Put the pan on moderate heat. When it's hot, place a few steaks, 3-4, along with some of the garlic and peppercorn on the hot pan and turn them over quickly as they tend to stick initially.

The juices (euphemism for blood) will start running. If you want your steak rare, you need to cook it for about 1½ minutes on each side. If you want it well done, keep pressing down the steaks so that the juices run and the meat gets fully cooked. A well-done steak will be 3 minutes to a side.

Serve the steaks hot, as soon as they are ready.

Rocket and Tomato Salad

For 6

Rocket – *500 gms*
Tomato, medium-sized, roughly chopped – *1*
Extra virgin olive oil – *4 tbsp*
Sea salt – *½ tsp*
Parmesan, grated – *1 tbsp*

Wash the rocket and dry in a salad spinner or paper towels. Tear into bite-sized pieces.

Just before you start grilling the steaks, toss all salad ingredients together in a bowl and place it on the table, along with some crusty bread.

Let the diners start nibbling on some good bread, extra virgin olive oil, finally topped off by the steak.

Mashed Potatoes

For 6

Potatoes, medium-sized – *6*
Salt – *5 tsp*
Butter – *4 tbsp/60 gms*
Milk – *½ cup*
Wasabi (optional) – *1 tbsp*

Scrub the potatoes, peel and cut them vertically. Place them, along with the salt, in a pan of water and bring to a boil. Once it's bubbling, turn the heat down to moderate and cook for about 15 minutes.

Drain the potatoes, mash with the butter and hot milk either with an electric beater or a potato masher.

If you like wasabi, add now.

show dinners

Mustard Fish 101

For 6

This is such an exotic dish with so many variations that I had to, absolutely, include it and some of its variations.

Mustard seeds – 1 cup
Salt – 1 tsp + ½ tsp
Green or red chillies – 2 + 2 + 1
Fish, ideally river fish – 1 kg
Turmeric powder – ½ tsp
Mustard oil – 1 tbsp + 1 tsp + extra to taste

Soak the mustard seeds in 1½ cups of water, with 1 tsp salt and 2 chillies for 20-30 minutes. Drain and pulse grind.

If the fish is large, cut it into pieces about ½-inch thick and 2-inches long. If the fish is to be kept whole, and are about 3-4 inches long, just trim them.

Wash the fish and pat dry.

Coat fish with ½ tsp of salt and the turmeric and let it marinate for 15 minutes.

Heat 1 tbsp of oil in a pan. When hot, fry the fish in batches, on each side for a minute. The idea is not to make crisp fries, just remove the rawness. Remove the fish from the pan and set aside.

Add 1 tsp of oil to the pan and heat. Slit 2 chillies and add them to the pan.

Dilute the mustard paste in water, and holding a strainer over the pan, filter it through. This I do to keep the rough mustard skin out and make the gravy smoother.

Once it starts bubbling, lower the heat and put in the fish. Cook for 2 minutes and turn off the heat.

To serve, pour the fish and the gravy into a dish. Swirl a little oil on it for a sharp kick.

Split the remaining chilli and the place it in the dish. This should not be runny like a curry, but just the fish coated in the mustard.

Variations

Tomatoes: After adding the mustard and before the fish, you could add 1 chopped tomato.

Coriander leaves: While serving, sprinkle the dish with coriander leaves.

Ready-made mustard: I have often used processed ready-made mustard, especially Bengali kashundi, instead of making my own paste. Just remember that ready-made mustard is processed, so it doesn't need much cooking.

Yogurt: Instead of diluting the mustard paste in water, use 1 cup of yogurt whisked with 1 cup of water. This doesn't need to be strained.

Vegetables: Steam vegetables like cauliflower, broccoli, cabbage or green peas. Mix the mustard paste and oil in and serve. Unlike the fish, the dominant taste here will be the vegetables, so for 1 kg of vegetables, 2 tbsp of mustard paste would be correct.

Aubergine: Fry slices of aubergine. Beat the mustard paste with 1 cup yogurt, 1 tsp sugar and 1½ tsp of garlic paste. Assemble this dish by placing a layer of aubergines in the serving platter and pouring the mustard-yogurt mix over it. Sprinkle some mint or coriander. This can be served at room temperature or even cold.

Steamed: If you get really fresh fish or prawns, smear it in the mustard paste and place in aluminium foil in a colander (or in a tight steel box), seal the edges tight and steam over boiling water for 7-8 minutes. You could mix some grated coconut in the mustard paste. Once the fish is cooked through, remove on a serving dish, pour some mustard oil on it and serve.

Meatball Khichudi

For 8

While khichdi in north India is considered food for the ailing, in Bengal it's called khichudi and it's celebratory. It's eaten at festivals, as a fun meal on rainy days, and overall, holds positive connotations of health and happiness, as opposed to sickness everywhere else. While mutton khichudi is common (and delicious), I first ate this meatball version at my friends Sromona and Ahitagni's place in Bangalore. They were surprised I hadn't heard of the famous Ajij-ul Haq khichudi. From them, I learnt of a Bengali recipe book by Renuka Debi Choudhurani. There's a footnote about the name of this dish – apparently the author's husband had eaten this dish at the house of a gentleman called Ajij-ul Haq. He was so mesmerised by it that when he returned home he described it to her. Through trial and error in her own kitchen, the Ajij-ul Haq khichudi was born.

I love saying the name as much as I like eating it. Meatball khichudi is not too bad either – apart from describing the dish, which is the prime purpose of a name, it has special significance for me. When I was in school, my late father used to call me meatball – no points for guessing why.

It's slightly complicated to cook and it's important to follow instructions closely the first time.

It's one of my favourite party meals – a rich, aromatic, robust dish that I serve with South Indian raita – any raita, which has a hint of sweetness, is good.

Khichudi

Whole brown masoor – ¾ *cup*
Fine basmati rice – *2 cups*
Oil or ghee or a mix, recommended – ¾ *cup*
Turmeric powder – ½ *tsp + ½ tsp*
Chilli powder – ½ *tsp*
Ginger, grated – *1 tsp*
Onion, grated – *1 tbsp*
Onion, large, minced – *1*
Shallots, minced – *5*
Cinnamon, broken into small pieces the size of a cardamom – *1-inch stick*
Green cardamoms – *8*
Cloves – *5-6*
Bay leaves – *5*
Garlic, crushed – *2 cloves*
Ginger paste – *1 tsp*
Salt – *1½ tsp or to taste*
Sugar – *1 tsp*
Green chillies, slit – *5*

Boil the masoor with 1 litre of water in a heavy-based pan. It should be firm to the touch. Drain and set aside.

Wash the rice in several changes of water till the water runs clear. This is important as it keeps the grains separate. Spread the rice to dry on paper towels.

In a bowl, mix 1-2 tsp of the oil or ghee with ½ tsp turmeric, chilli powder, grated ginger and grated onion. Gently mix this with the rice while it's drying.

Place a heavy pan on the hob. Add half the remaining oil or ghee. When hot, crisply fry the minced onions and remove on paper towels.

Do the same with the shallots.

Pour the remaining oil into another pan and place on moderate heat. When hot, add the whole spices, bay leaves and garlic, stir for a minute and mix in the dried rice. Stir this for 2-3 minutes or till the aromas of heaven start wafting in your kitchen.

At this point, add about 3½ cups of hot water, ½ tsp turmeric and ginger paste and stir.

Once the water comes to a boil, add the boiled dal, salt, sugar, green chillies and shallots and give it one last stir, cover the pan and turn the heat down.

After 15 minutes, uncover the pan. By now, the rice would have cooked. This shouldn't be watery. If it's still runny, cook uncovered for a few more minutes till all the water is absorbed. Remove from heat and keep warm

Meatballs

Mutton mince – 100 gms
Garlic – 3 cloves
Onion, medium-sized, minced – 1
Dried red chillies, seeded – 3
Ginger, chopped – ½" piece
Salt – 1 tsp
Oil for deep-frying

There are two critical aspects to this dish. First, the mince has to be super smooth. For that, you need to super blitz it in the mixie – along with the garlic, onion, chillies ginger and salt. It should almost be like a pâté.

Second, the size of the meatballs should be no larger than marbles. For this, you may need to oil your palms so that the meatballs roll off easily.

Heat the oil. In batches, fry the meatballs for not more than 2 minutes. As the meat is so finely blended already, cooking will be a matter of minutes.

To serve

Add the meatballs and the fried onions to the khichudi and serve it steaming.

Aubergine in a Garlic-Yogurt Sauce

For 4

I'm a fan of the aubergine. As children from a certain kind of Bengali family, no lunch was complete without a fried vegetable like potato or wax gourd or pumpkin. Aubergine was my favourite – slightly crunchy on the outside, tasting of the mustard oil it was fried in, with its own unique texture. About ten years ago, I came across Madhur Jaffrey's *A Taste of India* where she gives a recipe for baingan ka boorani from one of the aristocratic families of Bhopal – it really was a moment! Slices of fried aubergine, a quirky sauce of coriander, garlic and turmeric, a soothing layer of garlicky yogurt topped with crunchy fried onions – the sight, the smell, the taste – classy, exotic, delicious.

I make variations of this where only the aubergine and the garlic-yogurt are constant.

Large, round shiny aubergine – 1/½ kg
Salt – ½ tsp + 1 tsp
Oil – 1 cup
Onions, large, finely sliced – 3
Turmeric powder – 1 tsp
Coriander powder, home-made recommended – 2 tsp
Garlic paste – 1 tsp + ½ tsp
Yogurt – 1 cup

Slice the aubergine into ½-inch pieces. Sprinkle with ½ tsp salt and set aside.

Pour the oil in a pan for deep-frying on moderate heat. When hot, add the onions in batches and fry till they turn golden. Remove on paper towels to drain.

Drain out most of the oil, reserving just 3 tbsp and put it back to heat.

Pat dry the aubergine slices and place them in the hot oil, turning after a minute to evenly brown both sides. Remove.

In a bowl, mix the turmeric, coriander powder and 1 tsp of the garlic paste with ½ cup water and make a paste.

Fry this paste in the same pan for about 2 minutes on moderate heat – this is to get rid off the rawness of the garlic and the spices.

Beat the yogurt with the remaining garlic paste and 1 tsp salt.

At the time of serving, spread the fried aubergine slices on a serving platter. Spread the paste of coriander, turmeric and garlic evenly over them. Pour the garlic yogurt on top. Sprinkle the fried onions and serve.

Californian Green Curry

For 4

My friend Gauri Gill is a globally acclaimed photographer who went to school at Stanford University where she learnt to cook this very international, Californian, Thai-inspired curry. She has such intuitive appreciation for food that it's almost therapeutic to cook for her. She could drop in for lunch when there's just dull karela and kaddu and she'll find some hidden meaning in them. She's an open-minded vegetarian, a liberal foodie. I include her green curry as part of the one-course dinners. It's special because of the way she uses orange juice to cut the thickness of the coconut milk – there's a hint of coconut, but finally it's a light curry. It's fresh, fragrant and has all the colours of a rainbow. Gauri cooks like an artist – tasting along as she goes by, gently simmering the vegetables in the green sauce, adding things instinctively.

Lemon grass – 1 stalk
Oil – 1 tbsp
Ginger, grated – ½-inch
Thai green curry paste – 1-2 tbsp
Coconut milk (see my note alongside the recipe for khowswey, page 24) – ¾ cup
Carrot, broccoli, red and yellow peppers, green beans, spring onions, mushrooms, diced – 400 gms in total
Tofu, diced – 250 gms
Green or red bird chillies, sliced – 2-4
Lemon juice – 1 tsp
Orange juice – ½ cup
Brown sugar – to taste
Coriander leaves, finely chopped – 1 tbsp
Soy sauce – a dash
Salt – to taste

Slice the lemon grass root fine by holding up the stalk vertically.

Heat the oil and add the lemon grass followed by the ginger and green curry paste. Break up the lumps in the paste and add coconut milk.

Add the vegetables according to cooking time – carrot, broccoli, peppers, beans, spring onions and mushrooms.

Give it a stir and add the tofu, followed by chillies, lemon juice, orange juice and brown sugar.

This curry needs to be cooked gently. Keep on a low simmer. The vegetables should not get too soft, or the beans stringy.

Add coriander leaves and a dash of soy sauce. Finally taste and add salt if required.

Serve with steamed rice.

Soul dinners

There are times when someone calls you for a drink and you feel full after eating peanuts and a reshmi kabab. By the time you get home, you're peckish and wish you could rustle up a minor tummy-filler. Or there are days when friends just drop in for a drink, but the conversation gets deep and involved and you don't want them to go. You cook something easy and hot so that the party doesn't have to end. Then there are days when you are running on your energy reserves but you need home food – the recipes in this chapter are to that end.

Bengali Moong Dal

For 6

This is dal which is extremely easy but has a hint of the exotic because of the unorthodox use of bay leaves. It works well at parties too.

Husked moong dal (yellow) – 1 cup
Salt – ½ tsp
Turmeric powder – ½ tsp
Oil – 2 tsp
Bay leaves – 2
Cumin seeds – 1 tsp
Dried red chillies – 2
Sugar (optional) – ½ tsp
Ginger paste – 1 tsp
Ghee – ½-1 tsp

There are two ways to make this dal. Here's the optional first step:

Heat a kadhai and roast the dal carefully on moderate heat, stirring it all the time till the dal starts to turn slightly brown and lets out an aroma. Wash the dal in several changes of water.

If you're skipping the roasting, wash the dal in several changes of water.

In 2½ cups of water, pressure-cook the dal with the salt and turmeric for 5 minutes or the equivalent of one whistle. The dal should be cooked and the grains separate. You could do this in a covered pan too.

Heat the oil in a kadhai and add bay leaves, cumin seeds and chillies, followed by a cup of warm water.

When the water is bubbling, pour in the boiled dal and add the sugar, if you are using it. Once the dal starts to boil, add the ginger paste, stir and bring to a boil again. Turn off the heat.

Serve very hot with rice, after spooning in some ghee over the top.

Soul Masoor Dal

For 6

This is the food I'd want injected intravenously when I'm on my deathbed! It's light, wholesome, healthy, cooling and delicious. Should be eaten with rice and a twist of lemon.

Husked masoor dal (pink) *– ½ cup*
Green chillies *– 4 + 4*
Turmeric powder *– ½ tsp*
Salt *– ½ tsp*
Coriander leaves *– a large bunch/50-60 gms*
Oil, preferably mustard *– 2 tsp*
Kalonji *– 1 tsp*

Wash the dal in several changes of water.

Heat a litre of water in a pan, add the washed dal, 4 chillies, turmeric and salt. Cover and cook for 20 minutes on moderate-high heat.

While the dal is boiling, slit the remaining chillies. Wash the coriander leaves, pat dry and separate the leaves from the stalks. This dal is thin and green, so remember the coriander is not just garnish.

Heat the oil in a kadhai. When it starts smoking, turn down the heat and add the kalonji and the slit chillies. Once it stops spluttering, add a cup of warm water and bring it to a boil.

Add the cooked dal with the cooking liquid and throw in half the coriander leaves. Let it simmer for a couple of minutes. Check for salt.

Just before serving, add the rest of the coriander leaves.

Dressy Moong Dal

For 6

This is a most elegant dal, bursting with layers of flavours, good enough for a banquet. The best thing is this can be as dressed up or down depending on how hard you want to work. I am a bit of a shirker, looking for shortcuts in life all the time. One day, I decided to surprise my dinner guests with this complex dal – modesty aside, it was truly spectacular. There are a whole lot of optional ingredients in this dal.

Husked moong dal (yellow) – 2 cups
Salt – 1 tsp
Turmeric powder – ½ tsp
Green chillies, slit – 4
Potatoes, medium-sized, diced (optional) – 2
Oil – up to 5 tbsp
Cumin seeds – 1 tsp
Bay leaves – 3-4
Dried red chillies – 2
Ginger juliennes – 1 tsp
Yogurt, lightly beaten (optional) – 4 tbsp
Cumin powder (optional) – ½ tsp
Coriander powder (optional) – ½ tsp
Sugar – ½ tsp
Ghee – ½ tsp
Roasted garam masala, powdered – 4 green cardamoms, 3 cloves, ½-inch stick cinnamon

Heat a pan or kadhai and roast the dal carefully on moderate heat till you smell the divine moong dal aroma. Be careful not to burn the dal – this can happen quickly, so control the heat and stir often. The dal should have darkened, but not turned brown.

Wash the dal in several changes of water.

Boil the dal in 4 cups of water with the salt, turmeric and green chillies for 20 minutes. The dal should be soft but retain its shape.

If you're using diced potato, soak it in cold, salted water – the longer the better. Heat a kadhai with 4 tbsp of oil. Drain the potatoes and fry without crowding the pan till they turn a crusty light brown and are cooked through. Drain on paper towels.

Discard the oil and add 1 tbsp of fresh oil to the pan. Once hot (not smoking – to maintain the elegance, it's important not to burn anything in this dish; it shows), add cumin seeds, bay leaves, red chillies and ginger into the oil and stir it on moderate heat.

Add the yogurt, if you are using it – this will curdle almost immediately, but cook it till the whey separates and evaporates.

Sprinkle in the cumin and coriander powders if you like, and the sugar and cook this on low heat for 2-3 minutes. By now, the oil starts bubbling.

Heat 2 cups of water. Pour it into the pan. I like dals runny and always add water before I add the dal – I find when cooked dal is added to warm water, the grains remain separate and the whole thing amalgamates easily.

Add the boiled dal with the cooking liquid into the pan, and stir to mix. Bring it to a boil. Turn off the heat.

Taste for seasoning. There should be a hint of sweetness.

Just before serving, bring the dal back to a boil.

Pour into a serving bowl, add the ghee, sprinkle garam masala and serve.

Sexed-Up Leftover Dal

For 6

This can be done with freshly boiled dal too, but generally this is what I do to revive leftover, semi-congealed dal off the refrigerator when I have unexpected guests. Masoor is best, but it works with everything else – arhar, moong, urad. If it's masoor or moong dal you're cooking, it's best to boil it in a pan and not a pressure cooker. It helps to retain the form of the dal. If it's arhar/tuvar or chana, beat them down in a pressure cooker. Very few can resist the combination of hot rice and a thin, spicy, hot dal. Tried and tested.

If you're making from scratch

Husked masoor dal (pink) – 1 cup
Salt – 2 tsp
Turmeric powder – 1 tsp
Green chillies, slit – 3

If you're using leftovers, start from here

Oil – 1 tbsp
Cumin seeds – 1 tsp
Green chillies, chopped – 2
Onion, medium-sized, minced – 1
Ginger, minced – ½ tsp
Garlic, minced – 2-4 cloves
Tomato, chopped – 1
Coriander leaves, chopped – a large fistful
Ghee – 1 tsp

To cook the dal, wash it in several changes of water till the water runs clear.

Put a pan on the heat with 3½ cups of water. Add dal, salt, turmeric and slit chillies. Bring to a boil, cover and cook for 20 minutes.

If you're using leftover dal, you should bring it out of the refrigerator and have it as close to room temperature as possible.

Heat the oil in a kadhai or pan. When hot, add cumin seeds, turn heat down to moderate, and add the chillies and the onion. Stir this for 2 minutes, till the onion loses its pinkness.

Add ginger and garlic and cook on slightly high heat till the garlic browns a bit.

Blend in the tomato, increase the heat and cook the tomato till it reduces in volume by about a quarter and the contents of the pan are a jammy mass.

Pour in a cup of water and bring everything to a boil. Add the dal. If it's freshly cooked, it will amalgamate with the rest in no time.

If it's semi-congealed and from the refrigerator, the trick is to let it cook in the boiling water without intervention. The warm water will restore the dal far better than you will with your prodding spatula. Gently break the lumps, turn the heat down and let it cook till it breaks up and become liquid.

Check for salt. Just before turning off the heat, sprinkle the coriander leaves on top and plunge a spoon of ghee into the pan.

Variations

Add a few curry leaves and ½ tsp mustard seeds in the tempering for a twist.
Brown the onions separately and add at the end instead of coriander.

Garlic, Tomato and Cumin Dal

For 6

This is another winner – hot, thin, garlicky and tart. It's a one-step dal, made in one pressure cooker. Depending on the company or the hour of night, I bring out my Futura pressure cooker on the table and serve directly.

Oil – 1 tsp
Ghee – 1 tsp + 1 tbsp
Cumin seeds – 1 generous tsp
Garlic, finely sliced – 3-4 fat cloves
Tomato, finely chopped – 1
Salt – 2 tsp
Turmeric powder – 1 tsp
Arhar/ tuvar dal (orange) – 1 cup

Wash the dal in several changes of water till the water runs clear. Keep aside.

Put the oil and 1 tsp ghee in a pressure cooker and place on moderate heat. When it heats up add the cumin seeds, which will foam for a while.

Once the foam subsides, add the garlic and let it turn brown before you mix in the tomato. Cook this on moderate-high heat for about 3 minutes.

Pour in 1½ litres water and add the salt, turmeric and finally the dal. Give it a good stir and pressure-cook for 10 minutes on low heat.

If you have time, you can let the pressure subside. Or you can hold the pressure cooker under a thin stream of water from the tap (hold it away from your body and face) till the pressure goes down and you can open the lid.

Uncover and return to heat for a few minutes. With a whisk or a fork, stir the dal to make sure it's one homogenous mass and not islands of dal floating in puddles of liquid.

For good measure, a spoon of ghee can be used at this stage. It's sublime even without.

Eggy Pasta

For 2

This is delightfully easy and delicious – inspired by spaghetti carbonara, but a vanilla version, which doesn't necessarily need bacon. It lends itself nicely to a bottle of chilled white wine and some crusty bread. Eggy, creamy, cheesy, hot – what's not to like when you need a carb shot?

Spaghetti or fettuccine – 200 gms
Salt – 2 tsp
Eggs, free range or desi recommended – 4
Grated Parmesan – 1 tbsp
Milk or cream – 4 tbsp
Grilled bacon bits (optional)
Black pepper, freshly ground – as much as you like

Cook the pasta according to instructions on the packet, in 2 litres of boiling water to which you have added the salt. It takes 20-25 minutes to become al dente.

While the pasta is boiling, beat the eggs with the cheese and milk or cream – it shouldn't be fluffy, just smooth and creamy.

Once the pasta is done, turn off the heat and drain the water out gently into a bowl.

Fold the beaten eggs into the pasta to coat thoroughly. Add some of the pasta water from the bowl and mix gently. The sauce should be creamy – a mix of the eggs, cream and starchy pasta water.

Sprinkle bacon if you like, and grind some pepper on top while serving.

Sleep-Inducing Potato and Poppy Seeds

For 5

Posto or poppy seeds is Bengal's big secret from the rest of India – Bengalis eat vast quantities of it – as a paste with mustard oil and garlic, as crusty patties with dal, as a sweet chutney, as thickener in curries. It is an elegant, soul-satisfying ingredient which is hugely underrated. Alu posto – or poppy seeds with potato – is one of the most common ways of eating posto. This is not the traditional version, but my own hot and garlicy take on it.

Poppy seeds – 100 gms
Green chillies – 3 or more, I would use 5
Potatoes, medium-sized – 2
Garlic paste – 1 heaped tsp, from 4 cloves
Salt – ½ tsp
Mustard oil – 1 tbsp

Soak the poppy seeds and green chillies in a cup of water for about 30 minutes, if you have the time. Strain.

Cut the potatoes lengthwise in half and each half into 8 pieces. Alternatively, dice them.

Put the soaked poppy seeds, green chillies (break them up using your fingers into a few pieces), garlic paste, salt and some of the soaking water in a blender and grind it to a smooth paste, the consistency of hummus.

Heat the oil in a pan or a kadhai till it starts smoking. Lower heat to moderate and add the potatoes. Fry the potatoes till they form a light brown crust and are cooked through. You could cover and cook them so that they get cooked properly.

Add the paste from the blender and stir and cook for about 5 minutes. Some of the water will evaporate and the poppy seeds will turn a bit grainy.

Eat/serve with hot rice and more green chillies on the side.

Poppy seeds are known to be soporific, so don't plan a business meeting after this. Lovely on a Sunday afternoon, followed by a nap.

Eastern Egg Curry and Bread

For 4

I am a big egg curry fan – there's something about boarding school upbringing that I hold responsible for this personality trait. The only thing that you can count on in dreary hostel meals is often an omelette or a fried egg – and lifelong dependence and love is borne. The availability of eggs is never in question – even if you've run out, there's always the neighbourhood shop or the neighbour. I have rescued many a last-minute situation with this egg curry. It has lemon grass and galangal, which is fairly routine in Mumbai homes as we use it in our daily tea. If you don't have fresh, dried lemon grass is one of the magic ingredients, which should be in all kitchens prone to showing off.

Oil – 2 tbsp
Onion, medium-sized, finely sliced – 1
Garlic, finely sliced – 2 cloves
Coconut milk (see my note alongside the recipe for khowswey, page 24) – 2 cups
Salt – 1 tsp
Lime juice or tamarind water – 2 tsp
Eggs – 8
Mint leaves – a large fistful

Spice paste
Lemon grass, root and hard portions, minced – 1 tbsp
Galangal or ginger – 1-inch cube
Chilli powder – ½-2 tsp
Black pepper, freshly ground – ½ tsp

Soak all the spice paste ingredients in ½ cup of water. Grind to as a fine a paste as possible.

Heat the oil in a pan. Fry the onion and garlic till they turn translucent. Add the spice paste from the grinder.

Stir and fry for 8-10 minutes on moderate heat. By this time, the paste should have changed colour and the oil bubbling along the edges of the pan.

Stir in the coconut milk and salt and bring it to a boil.

When the curry is simmering steadily, take it off the heat and pour it out through a strainer. Clean the pan of any pieces of lemon grass with a paper towel, pour the strained liquid back into the pan and bring it to a boil again.

Once the curry is boiling, gently crack the eggs and introduce them, one at a time, into the pan of boiling gravy. With a spoon, pour hot curry over the eggs so that they cook uniformly. Turn off the heat when the eggs set.

Pour into a serving dish. Finish with a generous handful of mint leaves.

Serve with hot rice, bread or pao.

soul dinners

Toast Soldiers and Egg

For 1, always

My godson Ogu is a boy of nine who's a bit of a finicky eater. Like any other boy between two and 200, he cannot resist the word soldier. A soldier who's toast is even more fascinating. Little did he know that toast soldiers are just toast, cut up into strips. This was my way of stuffing some nutrition into him.

If you're a grown-up egg lover like me, this meal unfailingly hits the spot as I get back from work at night and dip one soldier after another into the glutinous half-boiled egg and finish off by scraping the leftovers with a spoon. You can't eat this meal unless you have an egg cup.

Egg – 1
Sliced bread – 1-2 slices
Salt
Black pepper, freshly ground

Bring 3 cups of water to a boil in a small pan. As the water starts bubbling, put in the egg and let it cook for 2-3 minutes. Turn off the heat, and place it under cold running water for a minute to stop it setting further. Remove and put it into the egg cup.

While the egg is cooking, toast the bread and cut it into finger-sized strips. It's important for the toast to be crisp or else the soldiers will fail in their duty of penetrating the soft egg for a proper dip and a stir. Place the strips (soldiers) on a plate.

With the back of a spoon, crack the top of the egg to make an opening wide enough for the soldiers. Sprinkle some salt and pepper.

Dip toast into egg and eat. As you eat, the hole will increase. Finish off by using a spoon and scraping the inside of the shell.

Cheese, Mustard and Onion Sandwich

For 1

This is one of the simplest sandwiches – for those with a mature taste. It has delusions of grandeur – every time I eat it, I feel a bit posh in a French kind of way! It's one of the most convenient packed lunches as well as a late-evening meal, especially with a glass of red wine, left over from an earlier evening. Not great as a romantic meal, unless you're deep into the relationship and no amount of cheese and onion breath will deter you from your path of true love.

Wholewheat or any other bread – 2 slices
Strong mustard, Colman's or kashundi – 1 tbsp
Onion slices – 4
Cheddar or processed cheese – 2 thick slices

Trim the crusts of the bread and lay the two slices on a chopping board. Spread the mustard generously.

On one of the slices, layer the onions and the cheese slices and cover with the other slice. Press it down and cut diagonally.

Serve with more mustard if you're an extreme person, or ketchup.

Farewell Chicken Sandwich

For 6 sandwiches

When I got married, my husband and I lived in different cities. He would drive down once in three weekends to meet me, and drive back early on a Monday morning. As a newly-wed, I took my wifely duties extremely seriously and packed him sandwiches for the journey and a bottle of watermelon juice which I kept in the freezer the night before. By the time he got thirsty, the juice would have melted and turned into slush. The sandwiches were a big hit. The trick is the home-made mayonnaise (page 136) and the best quality white bread.

Chicken on the bone – 400 gms
Celery, roughly chopped – 1 stick
Parsley – 4 stems
Onion, medium-sized, roughly chopped – 1
Garlic – 6 cloves
Ginger – 1-inch piece
Whole black peppercorns – 1 tsp
Salt – 1 tsp
White bread – 6 slices
Mustard – 1-2 tbsp
Mayonnaise – 3 tbsp

Put the pieces of chicken, celery, parsley, onion, garlic, ginger, peppercorns and salt in a large pan. Cover with cold water and bring to a boil.

Cover pan and cook for 15 minutes or till the chicken has turned white and is cooked through.

Once cool, place the chicken in the stock to cool in a refrigerator. This is important. The chicken needs to be cold or the mayonnaise will curdle. Given that the principal ingredients of mayonnaise are egg yolk and oil, it will become a club sandwich instead of a chicken sandwich. Leaving the chicken in the stock till you are ready to use it, keeps the flesh nice and succulent.

Spread the bread on newspaper on the kitchen counter and trim the crusts. If you like texture, keep the crust. Spread mustard on all the slices.

Take the chicken out of the refrigerator, extricate the pieces from the stock (strain and save the stock). Separate the flesh from the bones and shred the meat.

Mix the chicken with the mayonnaise. Check seasoning.

Generously spread the chicken on three slices. Cover with the other three. With a sharp knife, cut diagonally. Wrap in foil if you're packing it (excellent for winter picnics).

If you want to add to the volume and you don't have enough chicken, supplement it with slices of tomatoes and cucumber – the slightly sour crunch only adds to the pleasure.

Calcutta Club Chicken Sandwiches

For 4 sandwiches

When I was in college, every once in a while I used to rendezvous with my mother at her club – she after meetings and I after college. We would sit on the veranda by the lawn and share a pot of Darjeeling tea and a plate of these chicken sandwiches. Sharp mustard, soothing boiled chicken and good white bread – we often ordered one more plate.

Chicken on the bone – *200 gms*
Salt – *½ tsp + extra for sprinkling*
Whole black peppercorns – *1 tsp*
White bread – *4 slices*
Butter – *to spread*
Strong English mustard – *1 tsp*
Black pepper, freshly ground – *to taste*

Boil the chicken in a pan with salt, peppercorns and a cup of water for 10 minutes. Drain and cool, if needed in the refrigerator.

Neatly trim the crusts of the bread. Butter the bread. Spread mustard generously. Sprinkle with salt and pepper.

Once the chicken is cold, shred it. Place on two of the slices and cover with the other two. Cut diagonally.

I like to eat this with more mustard.

Fried Rice

In India, there's deep comfort in fried rice. Mothers showed off their Chinese cooking skills at dinner parties with a fried rice. The easiest packed lunch after sandwiches was an egg fried rice made with leftover rice. Eating at a Chinese restaurant would be unthinkable without ordering a fried rice. Only now we've become all posh and order steamed rice. I know all's well with the world when I eat a mixed fried rice in Kolkata – it has to have strips of egg, minute dices of pork and the smallest shrimps. It's always a little underdone and smells a bit raw and starchy from a certain kind of rice. It's not fried rice if it's made of fine-grained basmati.

For a good home-made fried rice, I have two rules:

1. Use leftover rice or precooked rice.
2. The rice should be a little underdone. It helps if it is not lumpy – fried rice should be free-flowing.

There are infinite variations of fried rice – I'm giving my favourite ones, which by now you must have figured, are easy to make.

Egg, Bacon and Shrimp Fried Rice

For 2

In an ideal world, you would have all three in your refrigerator. But since this chapter is all about spontaneous cooking, it's quite acceptable to use just one of the principal ingredients. The trick to this is cooking the rice in home-made chicken stock (page 84).

Oil – 1 tbsp + 1 tbsp
Spring onions, finely sliced, white and green separated – 4 stems
Ginger, shredded – ½ tsp
Garlic, finely sliced – 1 clove
Leftover rice – 3 cups
Salt – 1 tsp + a pinch
Shrimps, boiled – 3 tbsp
Bacon or ham, diced – 2 strips
Eggs – 3
Soy sauce – 1 tsp

Heat 1 tbsp oil to smoking point, add the whites of the spring onion and stir-fry till they become soft but not brown.

Add ginger and garlic and stir on high heat for 2 minutes.

Throw in the rice and 1 tsp salt and mix it in, ideally with a chopstick or fork. When the rice is heated through, put in the shrimps and bacon or ham. Let this cook for a couple of minutes.

Lightly beat the eggs with a pinch of salt and pour it over the rice. Turn off the heat. Stir the eggs in quickly so that they cook in the heat of the rice, but are still a bit runny.

If you don't care for runny eggs, you could always make an omelette, cut it into strips and add it to the rice. The trick for a really interesting omelette is to deep fry the eggs. It becomes crunchy and adds yet another texture.

Spoon the rice on to a serving dish or individual bowls. Sprinkle the green part of the spring onions and some soy sauce to taste.

Egg, Green Pea and Spring Onion Fried Rice

For 1

I ate this at a restaurant in Shanghai – it was so eggy that my friend couldn't eat it. I loved it precisely for that. The secret ingredient is organic, free range or desi eggs. It's a perfect late-night TV dinner, eaten out of a bowl by itself.

Shelled green peas – 3 tbsp
Oil – 1 tsp
Spring onions, very finely sliced, white and green separated – 2 stems
Capsicum, finely sliced – ½
Eggs, free range – 2
Salt – a pinch + ½ tsp
Cooked rice – 1½ cups
Dark soy sauce – 1 tsp

In 2 ½ cups of boiling water, drop the green peas for a minute and drain.

Heat oil in a kadhai till it is smoking. Swirl the oil around and add the whites of the spring onions. Stir-fry on high heat for a minute, followed by the capsicum, for a minute, and then the green peas.

Beat the eggs with a pinch of salt and pour it into the kadhai. Turn off the heat. As the eggs start to set, gently add the rice and ½ tsp salt, and stir with a chopstick or a fork.

Mix in green parts of the spring onions.

Eat out of a bowl after adding some soy sauce if you like.

South Indian Fried Rice

For 2

This is perfect as a packed lunch, a breakfast or an irregular, late lunch. It looks lovely – the white rice embellished by the colours of all that you add.

Oil – 2 tsp
Mustard seeds – 1 tsp
Curry leaves – 2 sprigs
Husked urad dal (white) – 1 tsp
Asafoetida powder – a large pinch
Green or red chillies, chopped – 2-4
Onion, medium-sized, finely minced – 1
Leftover rice – 3 cups
Salt – 1½ tsp
Lime juice – 1 tbsp

Heat the oil in a pan on high heat. Lower heat to moderate and add mustard seeds, curry leaves, urad dal and asafoetida and cook on gentle heat till the mustard seeds stop spluttering and the curry leaves are crunchy.

Add the chillies and onion and cook gently till the onion is translucent. To keep the rice white, it's important to control the onions and ensure they don't turn brown while frying.

Add the rice and salt and stir it with a chopstick or fork till heated through.

Pour the lime juice like a dressing over the fried rice and stir it in.

Delicious on its own, or with some cucumber raita.

Mushroom and Fried Onion Rice

For 4

This is a bit of a neither-here-nor-there recipe. It's not impressive enough to show off at a dinner party, but not too homely either. It's very easy to make with interesting textures (mushroom) and flavour (caramelised onion). If you have a one curry-type dish in the refrigerator or a spicy dal (like sexed-up leftover dal, page 68), you can take care of a full dinner with this rice, along with a simple salad perhaps.

Oil – 4 tbsp
Onion, large, sliced – 1
Mushrooms, sliced – 100 gms
Salt – 1½ tsp
Slightly undercooked Basmati rice – 6 cups

Heat oil in a kadhai or frying pan and fry the onion on high heat till it turns brown.

Add the mushrooms and stir-fry till all the water from the mushrooms has evaporated and they are wilted and fried.

Pour in ½ cup of hot water and some salt, followed by the cooked rice. Cook on moderate heat till the water is absorbed by the rice. Cool and separate the grains by raking it with a fork before you empty it into a serving dish or individual bowls.

It could take on stratospheric dimensions if you have a stock of mixed mushrooms like shitake, porcini apart from the regular local. If you're using dry mushrooms, soak them in hot water and use the water in the rice.

Fat Girl Gone Crazy: Fried Potato and Bacon on White Bread

For 2

There are days when I go to work and don't come back for a day and a half. When I return, I'm exhilarated having finished the task at hand and slightly high from the next few days of relatively no work. On such days (it's usually a Friday), a certain kind of recklessness sets in. We open a bottle of wine and in an act of complete daring I fry diced potatoes and bacon (pancetta if you can find it – it's available in Delhi and Mumbai) and settle into a kind of happy rigor mortis on the couch.

Bacon or pancetta – *200 gms*
Potatoes, large, scrubbed and kept unpeeled – *3*
Extra virgin olive oil or normal olive – *2 tbsp*
Parsley, chopped – *2 tbsp*
Black pepper, freshly ground – *½ tsp*
Salt – *to sprinkle*
White bread slices

Chop the bacon into cubes. If you buy rashers, cut them into 1-inch pieces. Cut the potatoes into small dices and soak in salted cold water.

Heat a frying pan and add the bacon. Turn the heat down to low and let the bacon bubble along.

When it's cooked through, add a glug of olive oil, wait for 30 seconds and add the potatoes. Let it all cook for 15 minutes or so till the potatoes are soft more than crusty.

Sprinkle in the parsley.

Remove with a slotted spoon on to a bed of paper towels before transferring to a serving dish.

Grind some pepper on top and sprinkle salt.

Eat plain or better (or worse) still, on good quality white bread.

Chicken Soup + Crusty Bread

For 2

This soup needs a bit of planning, but the result is so professional that it's worth it. This is a classic – you can serve it at a dinner, you can eat it when you're on a diet, but best for cold nights alone or in the company of a few others. You need nothing more than some thick toasts, if you're hungry. The trick is in the home-made stock. The secret is the use of a pressure cooker. I have grown up watching my mother boiling stock for eight hours. Away from home, I often used the pressure cooker. Only much later, I read Heston Blumenthal's – restaurateur and one of UK's most inventive modern chefs – column on gadgets in the *Guardian* where he writes about his amazing discovery of the pressure cooker and as an example of its magical attributes, cites stock-making.

My mother would not even hear of it.

Stock
Chicken bones, skin and other 'spare parts' – 500 gms
Salt – 2 tsp
Whole black peppercorns – 1 tbsp
Carrot, roughly chopped – 1
Garlic, top sliced off – 1 whole head
Spring onions, roughly chopped – 6
Celery, roughly chopped – 1 stalk

Soup
Butter – 1 tbsp
Plain flour – 1 tbsp
Chicken stock – 1 litre
Black pepper, freshly ground – to taste
Shredded boiled chicken (optional) – as garnish

Stock

Put everything in a pressure cooker with 4 litres of water and bring to a boil under pressure, turn heat down to lowest and cook for 45 minutes. Cool and strain.

Ideally, the stock should be refrigerated overnight so that the fat floats to the surface and can be discarded. If you don't have time, just strain and set aside.

Soup

On low heat, melt the butter in a frying pan. When it's bubbling, add the flour and mix it. Pour the stock into the pan, stirring constantly to avoid lumps and bring it to a boil.

Strain the soup and serve immediately.

I like mine with crushed pepper and a raft of shredded boiled chicken.

A variation by accident

I was cooking rice in this stock once. I got my measurement wrong and had to drain out the liquid. Thickened by the starch from the rice, it had become like conjee – divine with crushed pepper and a twist of lemon.

Kadhi, Chawal and Spicy Potatoes

I admit this will never be a meal I'll cook if I'm alone – but I resort to this when I have my friend Meenal over. There's something to be said about this wholesome and slurpy meal, which we eat out of bowls, that brings us closer. The kadhi is soothing and tart, the potatoes spicy – just right to balance off – and steaming hot rice. We invariably overeat because it's all so good – but rarely feel stuffed. Meenal always makes happy noises after this meal.

Kadhi

For 4

Yogurt – 1 cup
Gram flour – 2 tbsp
Turmeric powder – ½ tsp
Asafoetida powder – a large pinch
Green chilli paste – 1 tsp
Ginger paste – 1 tsp
Oil – 1 tsp
Mustard seeds – ½ tsp
Cumin seeds – ½ tsp
Curry leaves – 8-10
Jaggery, grated or sugar – 1 tsp
Salt – 1 tsp
Coriander leaves, chopped – 2 tbsp

In a mixing bowl, pour the yogurt and sprinkle the gram flour. Beat it into a smooth paste. Add turmeric, asafoetida, chilli paste and ginger paste. Slowly mix in 3½ cups of water.

Heat the oil in a kadhai or pan. Add the mustard seeds, cumin seeds and curry leaves. Pour in the yogurt mixture, stirring it constantly.

Mix in jaggery or sugar. Once it starts boiling, add the salt, turn down the heat and simmer on low heat. Turn it off after 5 minutes.

Serve sprinkled with coriander leaves.

Spicy Potatoes

For 4

A really basic recipe – but always a hit. The potatoes should be slightly crunchy. It's the lightly fried spices that make this so special – that and the crunchy poppy seeds sprinkled on top. Looks professional too.

Potatoes with the skin on, medium-sized, diced – 5
Oil – 1 tbsp
Cumin seeds – ½ tsp
Mustard seeds – ½ tsp
Chilli powder – ½ tsp
Turmeric powder – ½ tsp
Asafoetida powder – ½ tsp
Salt – ½ tsp
Poppy seeds (optional) – 1 tsp
Green chillies, slit – 3

Wash the diced potatoes in several changes of water and soak it for as long as you can in chilled water. Drain when you're ready to cook.

Heat the oil in a frying pan or kadhai. Once hot, turn down the heat to moderate and add cumin seeds, mustard seeds, chilli powder, turmeric and lastly the asafoetida. Stir and mix.

Add the potatoes and stir so that they are coated in the spices. Increase the heat and stir quickly for 2 minutes. Add salt.

Turn the heat down to low, cover the pan and cook, checking every 5 minutes. The potatoes should steam in their own juices, but if they start burning, sprinkle some water. Cook covered till done – this should be about 15 minutes.

Take it out on a serving dish, ideally with a lid. Sprinkle the poppy seeds, if you're using them, on the potatoes and place the chillies artily to offset the green of the chillies against the orange-red potatoes and cover with the lid (the steam from the hot potatoes will soften the chillies a bit).

Uncover at the table.

Alu Chhenchki (Potato Sauté)

For 4

This is also one of the unsung treasures of daily Bengali cooking – the chhenchki. I am told that the word chhenchki is onomatopeic – it resembles the hissing sound that vegetables make when they are added into the hot oil. I am a fan of kalonji and green chillies and use the combination when cooking several vegetables – potatoes being the most common, pumpkin, any of the gourds, broccoli. It's simple and satisfies a post-binge craving. This is the potato and onion version which we ate every Sunday at my maternal grandparents' – along with luchi (puffed, deep-fried puri made with unapologetic refined flour).

Potatoes, medium-sized, diced small – 3
Oil – 1 tbsp
Kalonji – 1 tsp
Green chillies, slit – 2-5
Onion, large, minced – 1
Salt – ½ tsp
Sugar – ½ tsp

Soak the potatoes in chilled water if you have time. Anything is good, but an hour is ideal.

Heat the oil and add the kalonji and chillies. Add the onion and stir-fry vigorously.

Turn the heat to moderate and continue frying the onion for about 3 minutes – by this time it would have browned as well as wilted.

Turn up the heat and add the potatoes, salt and sugar. Stir till the potato is coated with everything else in the pan.

Turn heat to moderate, cover pan and cook. Check every 4-5 minutes to ensure that the potatoes are not sticking to the bottom of the pan. If it's too dry, splash some water (not more than what fits in your hand) as you go along, till the potatoes are cooked. The chhenchki should be slightly gooey from the caramelised onions.

Some people sprinkle chopped coriander before eating. I find it perfect just like this. Excellent with paratha or chapatti, and a good accompaniment to rice and dal, especially the heavenly masoor dal (page 68).

Roasted Garlic Squeezed on Toast

For 6 tbsp

I love bread – it's my companion when I return from work late night and there's nothing in the refrigerator. The easiest thing I make is basic bruschetta (page 2). I could plough through an entire loaf by myself, standing by the kitchen counter. A slightly more interesting way of doing this is by roasting a whole head of garlic. Ideally, I do this when I have time and keep it in an airtight jar in the refrigerator. It's a fun activity.

Garlic – 6 whole heads
Thyme, fresh – 4 sprigs
Extra virgin olive oil – ½ cup
Sea salt – ½ tsp

Preheat the oven to 180°C.

Clean the garlic heads with a dry cloth to get rid off any mud or black soot. Chop each into half through the equator.

In an ovenproof bowl, place the garlic heads and the thyme. Drizzle with olive oil, sprinkle with the sea salt and bake for about 30 minutes, checking as you go along, adding more oil if it gets too dry.

Once the garlic is soft, squeeze the pulp out of their peel and mash it up with a fork or a mortar and pestle.

Spread on hot toast and eat. Or use it with olive oil and other spices to baste roasts, etc.

soul dinners

Scrambled Eggs with Spring Garlic

For 2

My first acquaintance with garlic greens or spring garlic (the shoot of young garlic) was at the street food market in Surat. It's a bit like chives, but broader and more pungent than sweet. Later, I noticed my mother-in-law using it as a garnish in a khichdi. She even made a delicious chutney with it which we ate with crunchy pakoda. My favourite way to use garlic greens is with eggs – either in soft-set scrambled eggs or as a topping for fried eggs. Garlic greens are available mostly in the winter. I have seen them in Mumbai and south Gujarat.

Eggs – 4
Salt – *to taste*
Butter – *2 tsp*
Garlic greens, finely chopped – *2 tbsp*
Chilli powder – *to sprinkle*

Beat the eggs lightly with salt.

Melt butter carefully in a frying pan – be careful not to burn it.

Turn heat down to low. Pour the eggs into the pan slowly, stirring gently with one hand and sprinkling the garlic greens with the other.

Turn off the heat while the eggs are semi-solid.

Serve on hot toasts with a sprinkling of chilli powder.

Prince of Good Times' Bacon Butty

The day job that affords me some of the exposure that has resulted in this book is as the executive assistant of one of India's most charismatic business tycoons, Dr Vijay Mallya. As part of my job, I have stayed on his yacht where the food and service are luxuriously impeccable. However, there are times – either after a day of hard work or a night of hard partying – when guests ask for something basic and simple. A bacon butty is one such recipe that is perfect for winding down.

The recipe below is Sidhartha Mallya's bacon sandwich. He had written down precise instructions for the crew of the yacht as to how to make it. I reproduce it verbatim.

As with most unpretentious food, this dish would demand perfection.

(Butty is a British slang for a simple sandwich. It consists of one central filler between two slices of bread. Bacon tops my list, followed by a chip butty – fat chips between white bread slices sprinkled with salt and pepper.)

Take 2 slices of bread (colour of bread will depend on individual choice).

Remove a bacon slice from packet and either grill or fry (again it depends on personal preference).

While article 2 is in progress, butter the bread

After bacon is cooked to desired preference (*), insert the bacon between the 2 slices of buttered bread.

Serve the bacon sandwich/butty to the person with tomato ketchup and HP brown sauce on the side.

* Preference will depend on type of individual consuming the sandwich. However, normally the bacon should be done in a nice crispy fashion, but not burnt or cremated.

eating
kday
kday
eating

92

weekday eating

I feel too self-conscious calling this chapter low-calorie or healthy eating as that would mean the rest of the book is full of super-calorific, cholesterol-busting recipes. The truth is somewhere in between. While the cheese and spinach pork in the Show Dinner (page 38) really does nothing for the body (don't be deceived by the mention of spinach) but takes the soul to the borders of nirvana, most of the recipes are cooked with minimal oil and with the best ingredients. It's all good.

This chapter is a tribute to unsung Bengali recipes that are bursting with health and beauty but too modest for cookbooks and restaurants. The Bengali culture of bhaté – literally translated cooked in boiling rice – is superlatively good for health. Traditionally, when the rice was put in the pot to boil, a few vegetables would be thrown in towards the end, which would absorb the vitamin-rich starch from the rice and get cooked at the same time. The rice would then be drained, the vegetables extricated and served as a first course with the steaming rice, a pinch of salt and a drizzle of mustard oil. Sweet pumpkins, bitter gourds, slithery okra, sharp radish mashed into the warm rice, with the rising fumes of mustard oil would unfailingly hit the spot. Now I have cut the carbs out – I boil the vegetables, dress them in mustard oil and eat them plain. Even those from the non-mustard oil cultures have been known to love vegetables cooked like this. Makes for a deliciously-virtuous weekday lunch with or without rice or chapatti.

During the week, I make an attempt to eat healthy to balance the excesses of the weekend. Most nights, it's an egg-white omelette, which I have grown to look forward to. By midweek, flagging under a waning will, I do a middle-of-the-road salad, slightly sexed up by using either one (but never all) of feta cheese, croutons, mozzarella (with rocket), but stop short at bacon.

Gota Shedho (Boiled Whole Vegetables in Black Gram)

For 4

This dish is an obscure gem of West Bengal cuisine. It's too lowbrow to be served at formal meals, therefore increasingly rare. There's also the unfortunate trend of sacrificing vegetarian dishes in favour of meat or fish, which has nudged dishes like this from the home menu as well. In any case, gota shedho is a niche dish cooked only among a few old-Kolkata families.

Like most vegetable dishes in Bengal, the season for gota shedho, which literally means boiled whole vegetables and dal, is spring, as the vegetables are required to be tender and small enough to be cooked whole in the dal. I haven't seen such an unusual and exotic mix of vegetables and textures in any other dish anywhere in the world – and one that is so easy to cook. Pungent radish, small, thin aubergine, hot dried red chillies and spinach are cooked in a slightly slimy dal with a dash of sharp mustard oil. It's a treasure waiting to be discovered by the world.

Gota shedho can be eaten with rice or by itself, hot or cold.

Whole black gram/urad – 1 cup
Salt – 1 tsp + ½ tsp
Tender, small white radish – 2
Small aubergines – 2
Whole dried red chillies – 6 or more
Spinach – 250 gms
Mustard oil – 2 tsp

Put a litre of water to boil in a heavy-based pan with a lid.

Wash the gram in several changes of water and add it to the boiling water, along with 1 tsp salt. Cover and cook for 40 minutes or pressure-cook it on low heat for 10 minutes after the cooker reaches full pressure. It should be slightly underdone.

If you haven't been able to get tender radish (not more than 4-inches long), peel and cut the big ones in half lengthwise and then across the width. Wash the aubergines and spinach. If the aubergines are large (more than 4-5 inches long), cut them into chunks roughly 3 x 2 inches.

Bring 2 cups of water to a boil in a separate pan. Add radish, aubergines, chillies and ½ tsp salt and cook for 10 minutes.

Bring the gram to a boil. Add the vegetables and the raw spinach. Cook for a minute and turn off the heat.

Swirl the mustard oil over the gram.

Eat hot, or pack and eat cold.

Boiled Vegetables

To me, the mental image that accompanies the term boiled vegetables is spears of beans and carrots bereft of any moisture (or joy) usually recommended by doctors. But the moment I stop thinking in English, I have visions of steaming pumpkin, radish, okra, even bitter gourd served on a bed of fluffy rice, with salt and green chillies on the side, doused in sharp mustard oil. These recipes are basic and perhaps not for a book, but ever since I rediscovered them, it has made my weekday lunches extremely simple, delicious and healthy. I treat these as salads more than cooked vegetables that are to be eaten with either rice or chapatti. Good hot or cold.

Boiled Pumpkin

For 2

Boiled pumpkin is my favourite boiled veggie – it brightens up my lunchtime by its sunny disposition. The bright orange is a proof of the vitamins it's stuffed with.

Red pumpkin wedge – 250 gms
Salt – ½ tsp
Mustard oil – ½ tsp
Green chilli, chopped (optional) – ½ or more
Onion, minced (optional) – 1 tsp
Coriander leaves, chopped (optional) – ½ tsp

With a sharp knife, peel the pumpkin and chop it in chunks or cubes.

Bring a litre of water to boil, add the pumpkin and salt and cook covered for 20 minutes. Pumpkin is a hard vegetable and lends itself well to pressure-cooking. It will take 5 minutes to cook from the time the cooker reaches full pressure.

There are two ways of eating it. The healthier option is with the water, like a soup after adding all the other ingredients. This is delicious and very filling.

I usually pack this for lunch. I drain the water and mash the pumpkin and all the other ingredients with a fork. During lunch, I open my lunch box, read a newspaper on the Internet and spoon the soothing mash into my mouth.

Boiled Okra

For 1

Boiled okra is an acquired taste for those not used to it, mainly because of its texture. In most cuisines, the test of okra is in its crispiness. Boiled okra is the antithesis – it's slithery, but sweet and delicious if you have bought the tender ones. It's healthy and excellent for constipation.

Okra, as tender as possible, trimmed – 4
Salt – a pinch
Mustard oil – ¼ tsp

Boil the okra in a covered pan in 3¾ cups of water for 5-6 minutes. Drain. Drizzle salt and mustard oil and eat. I'm afraid there's little else to do to sex it up.

Boiled and Mashed Potato

For 4

This is the queen of boiled vegetables. Different people eat it differently. In Bihar, mashed potatoes are called alu chokha – they are mashed with chillies, onion and mustard oil. For a school-day breakfast, Bengali mothers often give their children fena bhaat – a gruel-like dish of starchy rice with boiled potatoes and ghee or butter. Some mothers throw in a boiled egg to add some protein to the starch-rich meal. It's my happy taste of childhood. Even now, I often throw in eggs and potatoes (after scrubbing) into my rice to make a three-in-one boiled meal. Once the rice is done, I remove the potatoes and the eggs (with tongs) and mash them separately. The version here is the dressiest.

Potatoes, medium-sized, boiled and peeled – 6
Mustard oil – 1 tbsp or more
Salt – 1 tsp or more
Sugar – ½ tsp
Green chillies, chopped – 1 or more
Onion, minced (optional) – 1
Grated fresh coconut (optional) – 3 tbsp
English mustard or Bengali kashundi (optional) – 1 tbsp or more
Coriander leaves (optional) – 2 tbsp

Mash the boiled potatoes with a potato masher or fingers. Mix in all other ingredients. Divide them into balls and serve with hot rice or chapatti.

Boiled Radish

For 1

This is another sensational discovery, and doesn't come with the disclaimer like the two recipes above. Radish is seasonal (in India, it's a winter to spring vegetable). The best radish for boiling are the long white ones that look like a baby elephant's tusk. It's best hot with steaming rice, but quite fab cold as packed lunch too. And as always, it's minimal effort.

White radish – 1
Salt – ¼ tsp
Green chilli, chopped – ½ or more
Mustard oil – to drizzle

Peel the radish and cut into 2-4 pieces depending on the size. I like mine quartered if the radish is fat.

Bring 2½ cups of water to a boil. Add radish and salt. Cook covered for 5 minutes and turn off heat. Drain.

The radish can either be mashed with the mustard oil and the chillies. Or it can be eaten whole after drizzling some oil.

Boiled Bitter Gourd

For 1

This sounds much worse than it tastes. The trick here, like all vegetables that are eaten raw or cooked simply, is to buy the freshest and juiciest bitter gourd. This dish is quite bitter by itself and needs to be accompanied ideally by rice, or chapatti. Bitter gourd has fabulous dietary qualities – it's a remedy for diabetes and is an excellent blood purifier among other super healthy virtues.

Bitter gourd, tender – 2
Salt – a pinch
Mustard oil – a few drops

Scrape the scaly skin off the bitter gourd and boil the gourd in a pan of water for 7-10 minutes.

Drain and score the skin.

Eat with rice after sprinkling the salt and drizzling the oil.

Sautéed Spinach with Green Peas and Garlic

For 2

This is a traditional Bengali recipe, which I have incorporated as one of my weekly lunches. I have added a twist with the mustard. Again, it can be eaten with a sprinkling of rice or on its own.

Spinach, chopped – 400 gms
Oil – 1 tsp
Garlic, sliced – 2 cloves
Dried red chillies – 2
Green peas, shelled – ½ cup
Salt – ½ tsp *or fish sauce* – 1 tbsp
English Mustard or Bengali kashundi – 1 tsp or more

Place the spinach in a big bowl under running water. When the bowl fills up and the spinach starts to float, gently lift the spinach and drain the water and the dirt. Repeat this process at least 2-3 times till the water runs completely clear. Drain the spinach in a colander.

Heat the oil in a kadhai or a pan. Add garlic and chillies.

When the garlic starts browning, add the spinach and the green peas and stir-fry on high heat for about 3 minutes. During this time, the spinach will be giving out water furiously.

Turn the heat to moderate, add salt or fish sauce and wait for the water to dry up. Be careful not to burn the spinach.

Once the water has evaporated, turn heat to low and cook for a couple of minutes till the oil surfaces.

Add the mustard now or serve separately while eating. If you're eating it with rice and like heat, squeeze the juices out of the red chillies with your fingers. If you like it subtle, you may choose to omit the mustard.

Palak Dal (Spinach with Moong Dal)

For 4

Palak or spinach dal is pretty common these days, although everyone has a different version. The first time I ate this was a Madhur Jaffrey version from her book *Taste of India*, where she uses roasted paanch phoran – the five-spice mix common in Bengali cooking. The version that Mahesh Lunch Home in Mumbai makes is also delicious – they use puréed spinach, garlic and green chillies. I have two versions – one garlicky and green for everyday eating, and a more elaborate one for parties.

Husked moong dal (yellow) – ¾ cup
Dried red chillies – 2
Salt – 1 tsp
Turmeric powder – ½ tsp
Oil – 2 tsp
Garlic, sliced – 2 cloves
Tomato, medium-sized, diced – 1
Spinach, washed and chopped – 200 gms
Ghee – 1 tsp
Chilli powder – ½ tsp

Wash the dal in several changes of water.

Heat a litre of water in a heavy-based pan. Add dal, chillies, salt and turmeric. Cook covered for 20 minutes or till the dal is done al dente – the grains should be separate and firm to the touch.

Heat the oil in a pan or kadhai and add the garlic. When it browns, add the tomato and cook for 3-4 minutes or till the tomato has reduced and become somewhat jammy.

Pour the hot dal into the pan, followed by the spinach. Boil for a minute and turn off the heat.

Before serving, add ghee and sprinkle chilli powder on top.

Boiled Masoor Dal with Onions and a Glug of Mustard Oil

For 4

This is one supremely simple, one-step dal with an unusual combination of flavours. It can be eaten on its own, with rice or my personal favourite – hot chapatti. To me, torn pieces of hot home-made chapattis dipped in this dal is the taste of comfort.

Husked masoor dal (pink) – ½ cup
Madras onions, small – 12
Turmeric powder – ½ tsp
Salt – ½ tsp
Green chillies, slit – 3 or more
Mustard oil – 2-3 tsp
Coriander leaves (optional) – to garnish

Wash the dal in several changes of water. Peel and clean the onions.

Bring a litre of water to boil in a covered pan. Add dal, onions, turmeric, salt and chillies. Cover and cook for 20-25 minutes or till the dal is slightly mushy.

Pour the oil on the dal. Sprinkle with coriander leaves if you're using it.

Serve hot or at room temperature.

Boiled Green Moong Dal

For 2

This is a Gujarati staple that is traditionally eaten with kadhi and rice. Always on a lookout for interesting things to carry in my lunch box, I improvised it a little and started carrying this lightly sautéed dal to work. It's frugal, nuanced and nutritious.

Whole green moong dal – 1 cup
Oil – 1 tsp
Cumin seeds – ½ tsp
Garlic, sliced – 1 clove
Methi seeds – ½ tsp
Green chilli, slit – 1-2
Curry leaves (optional) – 6-10
Salt – ½ tsp
Coriander leaves (optional) – to garnish

Wash the moong dal in several changes of water.

Heat the oil in a pressure cooker and add the cumin seeds, garlic, methi seeds, chillies and curry leaves and sauté for a minute.

Add the moong dal, a litre of water and salt. Cook for 5 minutes after the cooker reaches full pressure.

Turn off the heat. Once the pressure subsides (either naturally or by holding the cooker under a gentle stream of water), sprinkle coriander, if you are using it, and serve.

A green mint and coriander chutney is a worthy accompaniment.

Tadka (Spicy Whole Moong)
For 4

This is a stunning dal, which originated on the streets of Kolkata. It's thick, dark, mooshy and exploding with flavours. Because it's primarily street food, the vendors often crack an egg into the hot dal to add more nutrition and taste, not that it's short on either.

It's served in earthen pots, which lend their own magic to the dish, along with soft, warm, spongy chapattis, quartered onions and green chillies. It's the gold standard of taste.

Whole green moong beans – 150 gms
Salt – 1 tsp + ½ tsp
Onions, minced – 1 + 1
Garlic – 6 + 2 cloves
Ginger, minced – 1-inch + ½-inch pieces
Ghee – 2 tsp
Green chillies, minced – 2 or more
Fenugreek seeds – ½ tsp + ½ tsp
Green cardamoms – 2
Cloves – 2
Cinnamon – ½-inch stick
Eggs (optional) – 2
Coriander leaves, chopped – 2 tbsp

Wash the moong beans in several changes of water.

Bring a litre of water with 1 tsp salt to a boil in a pressure cooker. Add the washed moong beans, 1 onion, 6 cloves of garlic and 1-inch piece of minced ginger. Cook for 5 minutes after the cooker reaches full pressure.

If you're not using a pressure cooker, cook the moong beans in a covered, heavy-based pan for 45-50 minutes. Cool.

Heat the ghee in a pan. Fry the remaining onion, garlic and ginger, the chillies and ½ tsp fenugreek seeds on moderate heat for about 5 minutes.

Add the boiled dal and let it cook on moderate heat.

In a separate pan, roast ½ tsp fenugreek seeds, the cardamoms, cloves and cinnamon for 2-3 minutes.

Crush the spices in a pestle and mortar and sprinkle over the cooking dal.

If you're using eggs, beat them with ½ tsp salt. Pour it into the simmering dal, stir and turn off the heat.

Sprinkle coriander leaves on top.

Baingan Bharta

I thought hard before including baingan bharta in this book. What's there to write about – mashed, chargrilled aubergine that is as common as dal-bhaat for most Indian cultures? There are very few things that are so easy to make, so exquisite and such a sure-shot crowd pleaser. There are degrees of bharta – a soothing plain one with just chillies and onion, one where the spices are built-up gradually depending on mood and energy, to the sublime one with yogurt and garlic.

The aubergines for bharta are known as bharta baingan – they are large (about 400 gms), dark purple and shiny. It's best cooked on a flame. Or else, you can grill it in an oven. Putting the charred vegetable in a paper bag is important. The aubergine sweats, making it easier for dry, burnt skin to separate from the wet flesh and to peel it. If you don't have a paper bag handy, omit the process. Just let the charred vegetable sit for a few minutes before you hold it under running water.

Basic Baingan Bharta

Aubergine
Paper bag

Place the aubergine on an open moderate flame. Leave it there till spots appear, for about 2 minutes. Turn it carefully using tongs. Continue turning till the entire aubergine is charred.

Carefully lift the aubergine with tongs and place it in a paper bag. Seal the bag.

After about 5 minutes, open the bag and place the aubergine under a gentle stream of tap water.

Carefully peel off the burnt skin. Try not to take off chunks of the flesh.

Baingan Bharta 101

For 2

This is the vanilla version, with a sharp mustard twist.

Aubergine, chargrilled and mashed – 1
Onion, minced – ½
Green chillies, minced – 2
Salt – ¾ tsp
Sugar (optional) – 1 tsp
Mustard oil – 1 tsp
Colman's mustard or Bengali kashundi (optional) – 1 tsp

Mix and mash all ingredients with a fork.

Best with fluffy, hot chapatti.

Baingan and Garlicky Yogurt Bharta

For 2

I dreamed up this dish (only greedy people have such dreams) one day and without trying it out myself, passed on the recipe with great authority to a friend. He made it, and said wonderful things. I like it because it's minimal, but has great chemistry and a few ingredients that work wonderfully well together.

Yogurt – 2 cups
Garlic paste – 1 heaped tsp
Colman's mustard or Bengali kashundi – 1 tsp
Sugar – 1 tsp
Salt – ½ tsp
Aubergine, chargrilled and mashed – 1

Line a strainer with a piece of muslin cloth. Turn the yogurt over it and allow it to drip into a bowl for a couple of hours or overnight in a refrigerator.

Once the yogurt is reduced, add the garlic, mustard, sugar and salt and whisk it till it's creamy.

Add it into the mashed aubergine and mix it till it's one.

Masala Baingan Bharta
For 2

I eat this dish in the middle of the week when I need a spicy pick-me-up, but don't want to cook something which takes too much effort or break my work rhythm by going out for lunch. The smoky aubergine is combined with onions, tomatoes, chillies and spices to make a hot, sweet and spicy dish that is dressy but easy to cook.

Oil – 1 tbsp
Cumin seeds – ½ tsp
Green chilli, chopped – 1
Ginger, shredded – ½ tsp
Onion, minced – 2 tbsp
Tomato, minced – 2 tbsp
Salt – ½ tsp
Coriander powder – ½ tsp
Aubergine, chargrilled and mashed – 1
Coriander leaves, chopped – 1 tbsp

Heat the oil in a heavy pan or iron kadhai. Add cumin seeds.

After a few seconds, add the chilli and ginger, followed by onion.

Cook on moderate heat till the onion has wilted and just turned colour.

Add tomato, salt and coriander powder and continue to cook till the vegetables are sweaty and the oil is bubbling.

Add the mashed aubergine in. Break the fibres as you go along so that it is one smooth homogenous mass. Once it's completely mixed, turn off the heat.

Sprinkle with coriander leaves and serve.

Salads

I go through salad phases. My salad days occur once in two years when I eat a nice big salad as a meal, but mostly I'm a salad-on-the-side kind of person. On the days I choose to eat only salad, these are my favourites.

> *Salad tip*
>
> Because salads are raw, it's important to use the freshest vegetables and the best dressing ingredients that you can lay your hands on. I save my best olive oil for salads.

Rocket Salad

For 2

If there's a leaf in this world that surprises me with its complex taste every time I eat it, it's rocket (rucola, arugula or roquette). It's also the most versatile salad leaf – I like to eat it in its simplest form dressed in my best olive oil and a twist of lime. Or I throw it in my house salad (page 35) which has millions of other things in it, but the rocket still holds its own. In between, I throw in crisp bits of bacon, shavings of Parmesan and most exquisitely, a ball of fresh mozzarella.

Rocket – *200 gms*
Extra virgin olive oil – *3 tbsp*
Lime juice – *a few drops*
Balsamic vinegar (optional) – *1 tsp*
Parmesan – *2-4 shavings*

Wash the rocket and soak it in iced water. Dry in a salad spinner just before eating.

Place rocket leaves in a salad bowl.

Swirl in the olive oil. Squeeze some lime juice and trickle some balsamic.

Place on plates and sprinkle grated Parmesan on top.

> *Variations*
>
> **Mozarella:** Serve fresh buffalo mozzarella along with the salad – a ball (50 gms) per person.
>
> **Bacon and Crouton:** Chop 2 rashers of bacon. Fry or grill. Toss croutons in the bacon fat. Mix it into the salad.

Caesar Salad

For 2

This is my favourite salad-as-a-meal. I first ate it in California in the mid-Nineties. This was before iceberg lettuce got its bad reputation for not being nutritious or tasty enough. Also before rocket became everyone's favourite exotic salad leaf. Restaurants made the Caesar salad with crunchy iceberg lettuce and bottled dressing. It was an unusual taste and texture. For a salad virgin, ordering just a salad was certainly a very grown-up experience.

The other reason I like Caesar salad is because of the croutons – not one for anything too healthy, I often have almost as many croutons in the salad as lettuce. I make my own croutons with thick, leftover bread rubbed with garlic. Also, for the sake of purity and health, I have started using some romaine lettuce along with the crunchy iceberg ones.

However, this is not a salad to be eaten on a day you're feeling fat. I use mayonnaise in my dressing, along with olive oil and Parmesan – none of which are for the calorie conscious. If it's any consolation, the croutons here are non-traditional too – they are without any oil.

***Romaine lettuce** – 1 bunch*
***Iceberg lettuce** – 12 leaves*
***Slightly stale French bread, multigrain bread or any other dense bread** – 2 slices*
***Garlic** – 1 clove*
***Parmesan, grated** – 1 tbsp*

Dressing
***Mayonnaise** – 2 tbsp*
***Olive oil** – 2 tbsp*
***Lime juice** – 1 tsp*
***Garlic, crushed** – 2 cloves*
***Anchovy fillets, crushed** – 4*
***Mustard, French or English** – ½ tsp*
***Black pepper, freshly ground** – 1 tbsp*

Wash the lettuce and soak it in iced water.

Preheat oven to 180°C and set it to the grill or toast setting. Place bread slices in the oven for 15 minutes.

Slice the garlic clove diagonally in half.

Once the bread is toasted, rub the garlic halves on the slices and cut into cubes.

In a screw-top jar, mix the dressing ingredients and shake till it's smooth.

Take the lettuce out of the water and dry in a salad spinner. For the success of the salad, it is important that the leaves are completely dry and crunchy.

Put the lettuce in a bowl, pour in the dressing and toss till all the leaves are coated.

Place the salad on the plates. Sprinkle grated Parmesan. Top with croutons.

Greek Salad

For 2

This is my friend Anubha's favourite salad because it looks so cheerful and tastes so fresh. Greek salad is chunky, crunchy, bursting with colours and flavours from the sharp feta cheese and the sweet and sour dressing. Perfect for an al fresco lunch, like the ones we eat at Sunny's in Bangalore.

Salad
Iceberg lettuce – 6 leaves
Tomatoes, medium-sized, diced – 2
Cucumber, medium-sized, diced – 1
Onion, medium-sized, sliced into rings – 1
Red bell pepper, diced – ½
Black olives – 10
Feta cheese, cubed – 75 gm

Dressing
Extra virgin olive oil – 3 tbsp
Lime juice – 2 tbsp
Garlic, minced – 1 clove
Oregano, dried – ½ tsp
Sugar – 1 tsp
Black pepper, freshly ground – ½ tsp

Wash the lettuce and soak it in iced water. Dry in a salad spinner just before eating and shred it.

Pour all the dressing ingredients in a screw-top jar and shake to mix.

Place the lettuce, tomatoes, cucumber, onion, bell pepper and olives in a large bowl.

Pour in the dressing and toss till everything is coated with it.

Top with cubes of feta cheese.

Apple, Celery and Rocket Salad in a Blue Cheese Dressing

For 2

I ate this for the first time at i-talia in Bangalore. The current chef, Mandaar Sukhtankar, has changed the eating preferences of Bangaloreans with his energy and innovations. He has a light touch and a deep understanding of Italian food. I ordered this salad from his seasonal, constantly changing menu. I was stunned by the fusion of tastes, perfectly balanced. He makes a big deal about sourcing the best produce.

Rocket – 100 gms
Green apple, cored and sliced – 1
Walnuts, lightly toasted – 3 tbsp

Dressing
Extra virgin olive oil – 4 tbsp
Celery root, finely diced – 1 tbsp
Lime juice – 2 tbsp
Blue cheese, crumbled – 30 gms
Black pepper, freshly ground – 1 tbsp
Water, to make the dressing runny – 1-2 tbsp

Wash the rocket and soak it in iced water. Dry in a salad spinner just before eating.

Put all the dressing ingredients in a screw-top jar, and shake it well till all the ingredients are amalgamated.

Place the rocket and apple slices in a salad bowl.

Pour the dressing and toss till everything is coated in the white dressing.

Place on individual plates and sprinkle toasted walnuts.

To be eaten immediately.

Egg-White Omelette with Herbs and Celery

For 1

Among several of my friends, an egg-white omelette equals food fascism. It means regimental eating, anti-fun and a way of life that is looked down upon by certain people. I could have been one of them, but I must admit that an egg-white omelette is one of my favourite weeknight dinners – it's easy to make, low on calories and cholesterol, has gourmet aspirations depending on what I put in it, and above all extremely familiar. From the most basic version of egg whites beaten with salt, made on a cast iron skillet, to the dressy one with herbs, these omelettes have great potential and are packed with good nutrition.

Oil or butter - 1 tsp
Egg whites - 3
Salt - a pinch
Parsley, chopped - a handful
Celery, chopped - a handful

Heat the oil or butter in a cast iron skillet or a frying pan.

Beat the egg whites with a pinch of salt.

When the oil or butter is hot, turn down the heat. Pour in the beaten egg whites.

Just as soon as the egg whites start taking a form, sprinkle in the herbs, cover the pan with a lid and turn off the heat. Leave it there for 30 seconds to a minute, depending on how you like your omelette.

The omelette will rise and solidify, and the herbs will get embedded inside the omelette.

Egg-White Omelette with Mushroom and Garlic

For 1

Oil or butter – *1 tsp*
Garlic, sliced fine – *1 clove*
Mushrooms, sliced – *1 cup*
Egg whites – *3*
Salt – *a pinch*

Heat the oil or butter in a cast iron skillet.

When it turns hot, turn down the heat, add the garlic and let it froth. Add the mushrooms, increase the heat and cook till they have wilted.

Beat the egg whites with a pinch of salt.

When the mushrooms are reduced and there's no more moisture coming out of them, pour in the egg whites, tilting the pan so that they cover the entire surface of the pan. Cover the pan and turn off the heat. Leave it there for 30 seconds to a minute, depending on how you like your omelette.

Masala Egg-White Omelette
For 2

Oil or butter – *1 tsp +1 tsp*
Green chilli, finely chopped – *1*
Onion, minced (optional) – *½*
Tomato, medium-sized, finely chopped – *1*
Egg whites – *3*
Salt – *a pinch*

Heat 1 tsp oil or butter in a cast-iron skillet.

Add the chilli followed by the onion (if you're using it), and tomato after a minute. Stir and cook on moderate heat till the tomato is reduced.

Remove the pan from the heat and transfer contents to a bowl.

Clean the skillet with a paper towel.

Beat the egg whites with a pinch of salt.

Heat 1 tsp oil or butter in the skillet. Before it starts smoking, pour in the egg whites. Tilt the pan to cover the surface with egg white.

Neatly place the tomato and chilli in a line towards the middle of the pan and roll the omelette like a pancake. Press down the omelette and remove from heat.

Jhaal Mudi (Spicy Puffed Rice Snack)

For 2

My weekday-eating chapter would not be complete without jhal mudi – a snack made with puffed rice (mudi), which is hot (jhaal). There are other Indian versions of this like bhel puri, but jhaal mudi is uniquely Kolkata. Vendors sell this on the streets of Kolkata from a drum-type contraption with many empty milk powder tins tied to the central drum. Each tin contains different ingredients like peanuts, cucumber, onion, chillies, coconut, a spice mix and chanachur. The central drum is the mother lode – it contains the mudi. The mudi man takes out a handful of mudi and puts it in an empty milk powder tin, which covers the mudi drum. Then he deftly pinches (it is a pinching action) out the other ingredients and throws it into the mudi. From a bottle tied to the contraption, he drizzles in a few drops of mustard oil and then in a furiously noisy action, starts mixing all the ingredients with a spoon. In impossibly small paper packets, he spoons in the mix and serves his customers.

The version at home omits the din and the cucumber, coconut and tomatoes, as they make the mudi soggy. It is a mixture of the chanachur (a kind of hot Mumbai mixture) or the chidwa and the crunchiness of the mudi, which is attained by dry roasting it. We get our mixture from Surat – it's called bhusu.

Puffed rice – 3 cups
Chanachur/chidwa mixture – 3 tbsp
Green chillies, finely chopped – 2 or more
Onion, finely minced – 2 tbsp
Mustard oil – 2 tsp

Heat a dry heavy-bottomed pan and roast the puffed rice, stirring it as you go along to make it crisp. This should be done carefully or else you will have burnt mudi.

In a big bowl, mix the puffed rice, chanachur/chidwa mixture, chillies and onion with a spoon.

Swirl in some mustard oil and stir (furiously) with a spoon.

Serve in individual bowls.

This has to be eaten immediately, or else it wilts, making the mudi chewy, soggy and no fun.

before and after

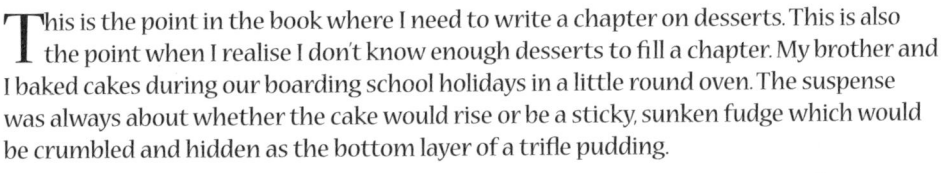

This is the point in the book where I need to write a chapter on desserts. This is also the point when I realise I don't know enough desserts to fill a chapter. My brother and I baked cakes during our boarding school holidays in a little round oven. The suspense was always about whether the cake would rise or be a sticky, sunken fudge which would be crumbled and hidden as the bottom layer of a trifle pudding.

Post employment and the convenient lack-of-time excuse, desserts were usually outsourced – urban India is full of delectable sweet shops selling rasmalai, kulfi, chocolate sandesh, rabdi, pantua, chandrapuli....There are ladies all over our cities who make a career out of supplying spectacular desserts on order. It would only be an ego thing to try and best that.

Now that I've justified my lack of sweet skills, I can claim to make up for it with my drinking expertise. I'm serious about what I drink – there was a time when the IT support guys in my office had set my password as rum-paani (I'm not going to explain). One of the sole reasons why I miss living in Bangalore is because you don't get Khoday's XXX rum in other cities.

While the thought of having a cocktail at a poncy bar is enticing, expectations are shattered quickly with a glance through the menu. Bartenders in India love flamboyant, sweet drinks which may include all or a combination of peach schnapps, lychee juice, Cointreau, tamarind water, blue curaçao, but it is incredibly hard to find a really kickass dry martini. While I bow to their originality, I draw the line and withdraw. And if I do manage to find a martini, and that's usually at a five star bar, I have to think twice – three martinis at a five star versus a month's EMI for a car?

In this chapter, I have listed some easy and flashy drinks I serve at home – and the few desserts that I make successfully, perhaps because they are extremely simple.

Before and After – things to drink before and eat after a meal.

Lemongrass Tea

For 2

Until I moved to Mumbai in 2000, lemongrass was an exotic herb used in Thai food. The day my husband and I were shifting into our new apartment, the neighbours sent us tea. It was almost symbolic for the first day of our new lives in a new city which uses hari chai ki patti – literally translated, green tea leaves, but in this case, lemongrass – routinely in its favourite drink.
For both the tea recipes, use average tea leaves and not delicate fragrant ones like Darjeeling.

Lemongrass – 1 stalk
Ginger, crushed – ½-inch piece
Mint leaves – 12
Tea leaves – 3 tsp
Milk and sugar – to taste

Put 2½ cups of water on to boil.

Wash the lemongrass and with a heavy mallet, crush its bulbous root.

Place the lemongrass, ginger and washed mint leaves in a teapot.

Pour boiling water into the teapot. After a minute, add the tea leaves. After one more minute, stir and strain into cups.

Add sugar and a few teaspoons of milk.

Cinnamon Tea

For 2

Masala tea is common – it's the safest tea to ask for while travelling in India – a sweet soup of spices, milk and sugar, with the tea playing a hidden part. The best I've ever had is at small wayside platforms in north Bihar served in baked earthen cups – I could eat the cup! Despite the spices, that tea had something fine about it – it was mildly spiced and sugared, the milk wasn't in it to make a statement and the caffeine from the tea had the desired kick. The first time I had cinnamon tea, it was made by my friend Simran – I thought it was clever to isolate one spice and use. She kept it subtle and refreshing.

Skimmed milk – ¾ cup
Cinnamon – 3 x 1-inch sticks
Tea leaves – 3 tsp
Sugar – to taste

Heat milk, cinnamon and 1½ cups of water in a pan over low heat.

Once it starts simmering, bring to a boil, turn off the heat and add the tea leaves.

Steep for a minute. Stir, strain into cups and serve with sugar handed around separately.

It is important to use skimmed milk if you want tea and not pudding.

Garlic Chhaas

For 1 tall glass

My relationship with this fabulous drink is through marriage. It's essentially a Gujarati peasant drink, which some of my husband's aunts made for me when I went to visit their farm. They used a small pestle and mortar to crush all the spices. It was a revelation. These days, this is my post-lunch drink as my homoeopath thinks I'm not getting enough calcium.

Garlic – *1 clove*
Roasted cumin powder – *½ tsp*
Sea salt – *a pinch*
Yogurt – *2 tbsp*
Ice – *4 cubes*

In a mortar and pestle, crush the garlic, cumin and salt and place them at the bottom of a cocktail shaker.

Add the yogurt, ice and 1 cup of water and shake it vigorously. When you open the lid, there should be froth on top.

Pour into a tall glass and drink. Or pour into a thermos and carry for lunch.

Sangria

For 12

This is such an exotic drink, so easy to make and perfect for brunches or sundowners. I like to make it in my biggest Tupperware box and stack it in my freezer for a few hours. At dusk, I go over to my friend Genesia's terrace and between her and her husband, and me and mine, we just keep ladling it into our glasses well after the sun has set, and walk back home a bit giggly.
In the tapas bars in Spain, sangria is served in a jug with a wooden spoon blocking the lip for those who don't want any fruit in the drink. I use only oranges and I cannot resist eating the steeped orange slices, peel and all. It tastes of spring. It's essential to keep it overnight in the refrigerator or in the freezer for a few hours.

Red wine (traditionally, it's a Spanish red like a Rioja) – *a bottle/750 ml*
Ginger ale – *2 cups*
Brandy – *¼ cup*
Triple Sec or Cointreau – *½ cup*
Oranges, sliced – *2*
Orange juice – *2 cups*

In a large bowl or a jug, mix all the ingredients, give it a stir and keep covered overnight in the refrigerator.

While serving, you could pour it over some ice and add a garnish of fresh fruit. I sometimes use a bit of chopped mint, but usually nothing.

Caipirinha

For 1

Caiprinha (pronounced kai-peerin-yha) is the kind of drink that grabs you by the throat – it's a drink from Brazil, and like everything else in that country, it shakes you up with its raw, refreshing sexiness.
This is a lethal drink, and if lethal is your thing, I suggest you buy yourself a bottle of cachaca (ka sha sa) – the sugarcane-based liqueur which has an intoxicating organic stink that gives you a bit of booze breath. What's not to love?
In Brazil, the limes are juicy and incredibly aromatic. In India, I use the usual lime and chunks of the heavenly gandharaj lebu that I get from Kolkata. This drink is given to excesses – for the total experience, you would need a lot of tart and a lot of sweet, a lot of ice, not to mention cachaca – you'll keep sucking at the straw till the last bit has been drained.

Lime – 6 wedges
Gandharaj lime or any other aromatic lime, cut into chunks – ½
Sugar – 2 tbsp
Cachaca – 60 ml/a large peg
Crushed ice

Place both types of lime and the sugar in a whisky glass and muddle it, dissolving the sugar and mashing up the lime with something wooden and blunt.

Fill the glass with crushed ice. Pour in the cachaca and serve with a straw.

Alternatively, you could make the same drink in a shaker, replacing crushed ice with ice cubes. Ditch the straw.

Dry Martini

For 1

If caipirinha's sexy, a martini is posh in an adult kind of way. It's as much for the powerful as for the arty. For me, drinking a martini at a bar fills an evening (or an afternoon in a dark bar with velvet curtains in New York) with possibilities. Martinis should be served in martini glasses – or else it would be too prosaic.
I include this recipe because it's such an easy drink to make, but almost impossible to find in bars in India – the trick for me is to keep the vermouth at a minimum. Vermouth is available at liquor stores in most large cities.

Gin (the best you can get) – 60 ml/a large peg
Vermouth – ½ tsp
Ice – 5-6 cubes
Olives – 2 or **a twist of lime peel**

Pour the gin, vermouth and ice into a shaker. Give it a few good shakes. Strain into a martini glass.

If you're using olives, stick them into a toothpick. Place either the olives or the twist of lime peel into the glass. (Use a vegetable peeler to peel the lime, then slice it lengthwise with a sharp knife – it should be as wide as spaghetti. When you cut the peel, it will curl; therefore the twist.)

Once the froth settles, serve.

If you want to be classy, frost the martini glass by washing the glass and sticking it into the freezer for 10 minutes.

This drink can be made with vodka as well – I like to call it a vodka martini, but I think it's called a vodkatini. Use expensive vodka for this.

Dirty Martini

For 1

I don't know whether I started liking this because of its taste or because of its name. But sometimes, at the end of the day, a girl needs salt and a drink, and that's when I order a dirty martini – a martini like the one above, with the brine from the olives. It's not a clear drink like the real martini as the brine makes the drink cloudy – which some like to call dirty.

Gin (the best you can get) – *60 ml/a large peg*
Vermouth – *½ tsp*
Olive brine – *1 tbsp*
Ice – *5-6 cubes*
Olives – *2 or a twist of lime peel*

Put all the ingredients except the olives or lime peel into a shaker and shake it up.

Pour into a frosted glass (see overleaf) and serve with the olives on a toothpick or the lime twist.

This too works brilliantly with vodka.

Cosmopolitan

For 1

For my friends and me, cosmopolitan became a rage after *Sex and the City*. I googled it and started serving it at my parties. The girls love it, and the boys, after initial coyness, can't resist it either. It's one of the few sweet cocktails I can drink as I use lime juice to cut through the sweetness of the Cointreau and the cranberry juice.

Vodka – *2 tbsp*
Cranberry juice – *2 tbsp*
Cointreau – *2 tbsp*
Lime juice – *1 tsp*
Ice – *5-6 cubes*

Put all the ingredients into a shaker and shake it up.

Strain and serve into a cool martini or other glass.

Bloody Mary

For 6

Bloody Mary is the comfort food among drinks. I have grown up taking sips from my parents' drinks at the Calcutta Club where my father would gently point at a napkin to wipe the salt from my mouth. While there are so many (and less painstaking) drinks to choose from on a holiday morning, nothing hits the spot like a perfect bloody Mary. The two things that are important for me are the temperature – I like lots of ice cubes in mine since it dilutes the drink as it progresses – and the second is to find the right heat level. The drink should give out some heat, but not overpower the sweetness of the tomato juice.

Lime juice – *1 tbsp*
Salt – *to rim the glasses*
Ice – *12-16 cubes + 4 per glass*
Tomato juice – *500 ml/2½ cups*
Vodka – *300 ml/1½ cups*
Worcestershire sauce – *1 tbsp or more*
Tabasco or green chilly sauce – *1 tbsp or to taste*
Celery stalk – *1 per glass*

Chop off a slice from the lime. Take each glass and wipe the rim with the lime slice. Pour some table salt on a saucer, put the rims of the glasses into the salt and shake off the excess.

Put 12-16 ice cubes in a jug and add all the ingredients except the celery. Stir with a non-metallic spoon (a metallic spoon will react with the tomato juice).

Place 4 ice cubes in each glass. Pour the drink into them. Stick a celery stalk into each glass. Cheers.

Phirni (Rice Custard)

For 6

This book will be incomplete without mentioning Thakur – our cook in Kolkata, Nishakar Patra, who is the best cook I know. What sets him apart is his extremely scientific approach to food (which he's thankfully oblivious to) that makes his food professional, but joyful and fun as well. He understands the process and is extremely innovative – in the three decades he's cooked for us there's never been a bad meal. His alu and dal parathas are legendary – translucent discs so sublime that they defy recipe. His phirni, however, can be reproduced with minimal effort. He ate it at Kolkata's many Muslim restaurants and came home and made it, set exactly like they do in the biryani restaurants – in flat earthen bowls.

Rice – 125 gms
Saffron – ½ tsp
Full fat milk – ¼ cup + 1 litre + ¾ cup
Sugar – 125 gms
Kewda water – 1 tbsp

Soak the rice in cold water for an hour. Drain and spread on kitchen towels or newspapers to dry completely.

Soak the saffron in ¼ cup of warm milk.

While the rice is drying, heat a litre of milk in a large pan on low heat, stirring periodically. This is the hard part – a good phirni starts when the milk has reduced to almost half its original volume.

Take the dry rice and pulse grind – it shouldn't be fine at all. The grains should be separate, smaller than couscous and larger than semolina. Stir the ground rice into ¾ cup of milk. This prevents the rice from becoming lumpy when you eventually add it to the reduced milk.

Add the sugar, ground rice with the milk into the reduced milk. Stir continuously on low heat for 4-5 minutes. Turn off the heat.

Stir in the kewda water and saffron with its soaking liquid.

While hot, pour into individual bowls to set.

It would be really classy if you can get earthen bowls – the pleasure of scraping off glutinous phirni from the sides of an earthen bowl reminds me of the monsoon – the first rain on dry ground.

Caramel Custard

For 6

When I was growing up, the synonym for pudding was caramel custard. I guess it's the quivering texture, the aroma of eggs and vanilla and the burnt taste of caramel that keeps it on the popularity charts for generations. This recipe is my mother's.
I make mine in a pressure cooker. It takes 5 minutes on full pressure.

Full fat milk - 1 litre
Vanilla pod - 1 or essence/extract - ½ tsp
Sugar - 100 gms + 2 tbsp
Eggs - 4

If you're using a vanilla pod, split it open with a sharp knife, scrape out the extract and add it to the milk. Bring the milk to a simmer, stir occasionally till it reduces by about half. Cool the milk. (My brother, who's a caramel custard freak, cheats all the time and doesn't bother to thicken the milk as much.)

In a blender, add the thickened milk, 100 gms of sugar, the eggs and vanilla essence or extract if you're using it and blend for almost 2 minutes.

Put 2 tbsp of sugar in a two-litre pudding basin with a fitted lid or a metal box with a fitted lid and hold it over low heat. The sugar will start melting, bubbling and burning in that order. Just as it starts changing colour, but is still runny, swirl the basin to coat the bottom with the caramel. Pour the milk mixture into it. Close the lid.

Gently place the pudding basin into a pressure cooker, ideally on a steaming stand if you have one. Pour enough water to come halfway up the basin.

Close the cooker and place it over high heat. Once the pressure builds up, cook for 5 minutes. Turn off the heat and cool completely. Refrigerate.

Before serving, open the lid and put a plate over the basin. Turn over. Some of the liquid will run. Cut in wedges and serve.

Chocolate Fondant

For 6

I feel there is an overkill of chocolate desserts in the market, so if I make pudding at all, I try and do something which is not easy to get off-the-shelf but popular – like stewed fruit (page 129) or a caramel custard (page 125).
Chocolate fondant or chocolate mud pie or lava cake is an exception. Few desserts can beat the drama of hot oozing chocolate against a mound of vanilla ice cream. My secret ingredient is the grated orange peel and the Cointreau. Remember, while you can prepare the batter and keep it in the refrigerator in advance, you can only start baking them when guests are eating their main course.

Good quality chocolate (70 per cent cocoa) – *150 gms*
Butter, at room temperature – *100 gms*
Eggs – *4*
Sugar – *150 gms (¾ cup)*
Flour – *75 gms (½ cup)*
Orange, grated zest – *1*
Cointreau – *a capful*

Grease 10 large muffin tins if you have them, or small stainless steel katoris – ideally they should be the same size for uniform baking, but sometimes it's interesting to use mixed sizes as different people may want different sizes. But it needs a bit of practice to know when each one is done. You could also use white espresso cups which saves you from turning the cakes over, but while that's stylish, I find it's not half as dramatic.

Break the chocolate into small pieces and mix with the butter in a bowl that fits tightly over a pan of steaming (but not bubbling) water. Beat and it will melt and amalgamate. Stir in the orange zest and Cointreau.

Beat the eggs with the sugar till well mixed.

Fold in the flour and then the chocolate butter.

Pour into individual tins or cups. If you're going to make it later, cover with cling film and refrigerate, to be taken out about an hour before eating.

Preheat oven to 180°C.

Once the oven is hot, put in the tins and bake for 8-12 minutes. While the outside should have hardened, the inside must be gooey.

To check, run a clean knife along the edge: it should come out clean. Plunge it in the centre of the fondant and it shouldn't.

Take the moulds out of the oven. Gently turn them over on to individual plates. If you're serving in the espresso cups, place them on plates. Dust the top with icing sugar – you can hold a grater over the individual mounds while sprinkling the sugar to get a perforated design.

Serve with vanilla ice cream, or vanilla and chocolate ice cream and candied orange peel (page 134).

If you don't like orange, replace the orange peel and the Cointreau with powdered cinnamon, grated nutmeg, a spoon of crème de menthe, instant coffee powder or a tablespoon of strong espresso for added flavour.

Orange Almond Cake

For an 8-inch round cake

This is the only recipe in the entire book I have had pangs to part with. It's my trump card and epitomises my kind of cooking. It's exotic (originally Tunisian), yet requires minimal effort (you don't even have to preheat the oven). I chanced upon it at a food court in London and I was stunned by its sensuousness – it's a moist cake with a slightly grainy, dense texture, an amazing synthesis of ground almonds, fragrant orange zest and eggs, slightly chewy and completely irresistible – with a sudden burst of spiciness from the cloves, more than the cinnamon. This is the kind of food I love to cook, and eat.

Cake
Breadcrumbs – 50 gms
Oil (sunflower or any other brand) – 200 ml
Eggs – 4
Castor sugar – 200 gms
Almonds, powdered – 100 gms
Baking powder – 1½ tsp
Orange, grated zest – 1
Lime, grated zest – ½

Syrup
Orange juice – 1 orange
Lime juice – ½ lime
Cinnamon – 1" stick
Cloves – 2

Mix all cake ingredients, ideally with an electric beater.

Pour the batter into a greased 8" round cake tin.

Set the oven to 180°C and put in the cake tin. Bake for 45 minutes.

It is done when a skewer or a knife inserted into the middle of the cake comes out clean.

Cool in the tin for 5 minutes.

Turn the cake out and put it on a wire rack to cool.

Heat the orange and the lime juices in a pan. Add the spices and cook over low heat for about 5 minutes till you get the aroma of the spices.

Put the cake on a plate and poke some holes into it. Pour the juices with the spices till the cake soaks it all in.

Serve warm or cold with cream or ice cream.

Stewed Pears in Red Wine
For 6

In India, desserts with fruit are dominated by the mango – its easy texture and strong taste and our prenatal association with the fruit can never go wrong. It's not an Indian thing to do any other fruit – we like to eat them raw.
Stewed fruits are a European thing. I love this – the pears are still hard, the wine thick, spicy and caramelised. Serve with cream more than ice cream. It needs the fat floating on top.

Pears, small, tight recommended – 8
Vanilla pod – 1 or *extract at a crunch* – ½ tsp
Red wine – 1 bottle/750 ml
Sugar – 100 gms (½ cup)
Cinnamon – 4 x 1" sticks

Peel the pears, but retain the stalk. Cut each pear vertically into two.

Split the vanilla pod with a sharp knife and scrape out the extract.

Put all the ingredients into a heavy-based pan. Stir everything well so that the fruits are adequately submerged.

Cover and cook on a simmer for 20 minutes or so, stirring occasionally. The pears should soften but retain adequate bite.

Cool and refrigerate.

Serve with cream.

You can also use peaches in this recipe.

Vanilla Coffee

For 2

The proof of a really good dinner is not just in the eating, but in what people do after that. I know a party's a hit when guests lounge around on the sofas, finishing their drinks over conversation. My friend Supratik always does the right thing and offers espresso (and milk and hot water on the side) or jasmine tea. I'm lazier than he is. I offer just coffee because that's what I like to drink after a good dinner. Vanilla coffee is not just for after dinner. It's for any time.

Ground coffee beans – 4 heaped tsp
Vanilla pod – ½
Milk, cream or sugar – to serve

For this, it's ideal to use a French coffee press or my home-made style which I learnt from one of our office boys.

If you're using the French press, put the ground coffee and the vanilla pod which should have been split with a sharp knife into the French press and pour 2½ cups of boiling water into it. Fix the lid and take it to the table. Plunge the lid after about 2 minutes. Pour into cups.

If you don't have a French press, put the ground coffee and the split vanilla pod into a coffee pot (ideally if you're going to bring it out on the table) or a teapot. Pour 2½ cups of boiling water into it and cover. After 2 minutes, stir and strain into cups.

If you like the professional frothy look, splash a generous handful of water on the hot coffee.

Serve the sugar, milk or cream separately.

Irish Coffee

For 4

It's only after a really successful dinner that I'm motivated to make Irish coffee – if you can pull it off, there's high praise at the end of it.

Ground coffee beans – *8 heaped tsp*
Sugar (optional) – *2 tbsp*
Whisky – *8 tbsp*
Cream and sugar – *to serve*

Make the black coffee as in the recipe for vanilla coffee (opposite page), using 5 cups of water, but omit the vanilla.

If you're really energetic, you could make caramel by heating 2 tbsp of sugar in a small pan and when it turns brown but still bubbling, dip the rim of the cups or serving glasses to caramelise the rims. It cools in a second.

Pour 2 tbsp of whisky into each cup followed by the hot coffee. Top with good cream. Serve with sugar on the side.

132

Cool Kitchen essentials

How do I define this chapter? Loosely, I have tried to make a list of gadgets and food that make eating better and simpler. This list may be a bit whimsical and subjective – based on shallow research findings conducted only among my friends. I have taken for granted that most kitchens have the essential essentials – burners, oven, mixer-grinder, refrigerator, basic spices and have added certain things that I believe add convenience, class and a bit of glamour to the kitchen, giving regular home food a professional finish. Some of the things listed – like ginger and garlic pastes – are far from classy, but extremely helpful especially for Indian cooking. Then there are things like candied orange peel, which by no means is essential in any kitchen – but on the day that you only have vanilla ice cream in your refrigerator, this is what will differentiate between a domestic goddess (gender-neutral term) and a hapless homemaker.

Candied orange peel: I use a sprinkling of this in chocolate cakes, hot chocolate fondant and serve it with ice creams. It's sublime and stays for years in the refrigerator. It's not worth the effort if you're going to use the peel of less than a dozen oranges for this. Remove the peel from the oranges. Place in a pan and cover with cold water. Bring to a boil, lower heat and cook slowly till soft; drain. Remove the white pith with a spoon (leave some white) and cut in thin strips. Put 1 cup sugar, ½ cup water and peel in a pan. Cook till the bubbling stops. Drain if any syrup is left. Cool on a wire rack. When it's completely dry, roll in caster sugar and store in an airtight container in the refrigerator.

Cast iron casserole: A heavy cast iron pan is very useful for cooking anything that needs slow and persistent cooking. Great for stews, slow-cooked dal, kheer. The enamel-coated branded ones like Le Creuset are now available in India, but they are expensive. At a pinch, a good old heavy pressure cooker will do the job.

Chopsticks: Chopsticks are high on fun, not so great on utility, but I love to serve steamed prawns or fried rice and other Chinese-inspired dishes with chopsticks.

Citrus reamer: I see my friends abroad use this. You just impale a lime or some other hard citrus fruit with the reamer and twist it in – the juice pours out with no fuss at all. You can use as much of the juice as you like and save the rest for natural safekeeping in its own skin.

Cocktail shaker: I think a crisp, dry martini is a sign of class, and while some people prefer it stirred, I think it's too effete without the froth that comes after a good shake; high on the cool quotient at cocktail hour.

Coconut milk: It comes in packets or cans, as powder or liquid and can change the complexion of a dish from the ordinary to the exotic. A normal mongrel-type curry can become Syrian Christian or Thai with a hassle-free squirt out of a packet. Boil rice in equal portions of coconut milk and water with chunks of pineapple in it; easy and special.

Coffee maker: If you're a serious coffee drinker like I am, and like the ritual of coffee-making as much as drinking it, a coffee maker is recommended. There is endless debate over which one's best – whether it's a French press, an Italian stove top, an American-style filter or an espresso machine. I find the espresso machine best for cappuccino, the French Press for espresso, the American-style coffee pot is good for those who like to have many cups of coffee through the day, not necessarily strong. The Italian coffee maker is also good for a thicker and a stronger brew.

Corkscrew: Many a party is ruined without a reliable corkscrew. While plenty is written about the rabbit wine opener, most beloved by bartenders because it's extremely sturdy, get one that will not embarrass you after you've had a few glasses and you need to struggle with the opener and the bottle held between your legs. Having said that, I just heard that Peugeot has come up with an electronic corkscrew – you touch the cylindrical device to the top of a wine bottle, press a button and voila! On my wish list.

Digital kitchen scales: This is the gadget to reduce your margin of baking error – a precise machine, which lays the base for the best cakes. After years of slightly vague cup measures, I feel like a pro using these scales. Also great if you're on a restricted diet as you can weigh everything that you eat. You'll be surprised how off-the-mark we tend to be.

Dried herbs: My purist friends think dried herbs is like putting straw bits in food. I disagree. The trick is to buy them from reputable stores – a sprinkling can lift an average meal to a special, nuanced one. Thyme, rosemary and curry leaves are especially good.

Eggs: Delicious emergency food.

Fish sauce: Thai, Vietnamese and other South East Asian cuisines use fish sauce instead of salt. All over South East Asia, it's available in restaurants and homes as a condiment. It's made from fermented fish, therefore it is intense in flavour and smell. I use it to make dipping sauces with chopped chillies, in curries (try with pumpkin, garlic and coconut milk) and as a salt-substitute in all kinds of things. If you develop a taste for it, you'll be hooked.

Garlic paste: This is the most utilitarian item in my refrigerator. In terms of utility, garlic is extremely versatile, lending itself to cuisines across the globe. There are days when I come back ravenous and eat toasts smeared with garlic paste and olive oil. While I'm all for outsourced ingredients, I have yet to come across commercial garlic paste that doesn't smell like paint – or something not quite garlic. On a day I have little to do, I peel about 250 gms of garlic and blitz in with salt and oil or water. This lasts about three weeks. If I had to choose one ingredient that I couldn't do without, it would be garlic paste.

Ginger paste: Not as important as the one above, but extremely useful in Indian and Asian-inspired cooking. Just peel 250 gms and blitz with a teaspoon of salt and about 3 tbsp of water.

Heavy-duty non-stick frying pan: Everyone has a non-stick pan but note the two critical words here 'heavy-duty'. The pan should literally be heavy (made with cast iron) and not some tin pan, which are commonly available. In India, a brand not known for its non-stick cookware is Hawkins Futura. They are sturdy, aesthetic and long lasting. Excellent for frying fish, making pancakes and dosa.

Ice: A difference between a good and an average party could be ice, especially in a hot country like India. A useful party trick is to empty ice trays into a large plastic bag kept in the freezer as often as you can. Makes a difference.

Knives: A majority of chefs cannot be wrong when they say if they had to choose a single kitchen gadget, it would be a good knife. Get one – it makes everything smoother.

Mayonnaise, homemade: I haven't yet found a really excellent quality off-the-shelf mayo in India, so I make my own. It's a velvety, versatile sauce which I eat with mashed potatoes, boiled chicken, steamed prawns and as a late-night snack, spread on bread.

For many years I was a failed mayo maker till I read somewhere that the secret to the perfect emulsion is that all the ingredients must be at the same temperature. Before this, the cold eggs from the refrigerator clashed with the warmish oil outside, resulting in bad chemistry and curdled gloop (which someone told me was an excellent mask for dry hair). I now use an electric beater or a silicone whisk with a hundred per cent success rate.

Use two egg yolks, 200 ml oil (I use sunflower or any other refined oil, some use olive) and juice of half a lime. In a clean bowl, place the yolks and whisk or beat on low speed. Slowly pour drops of oil into the egg and continue to beat. This is the challenging part as, after a point, your arms start hurting. Take a break, but don't get tempted to increase the drops of oil to a trickle until the mix has thickened in mass and lightened in colour. Continue pouring the oil. In about 15 minutes, you will notice the mayonnaise is coming off the sides of the bowl. To test, put in a knife – it should come out clean. Stir in the lime juice. Now you have your basic mayonnaise – add salt and freshly ground pepper, and mustard if you want it sharp, or garlic paste if you're using it for a dressing.

Motorised pepper mill: My friends are shocked I added this as an essential, and attribute it to my childishness and vanity (since I have one and

cool kitchen essentials

they don't). This is most fun – hold this on top of a fried egg, press a button and unleash a blitz of the freshest pepper. My gizmo turns on its own little torchlight – lest I start peppering the ice cream during a midnight refrigerator raid. Delightful.

Mustard: Purists will recommend English mustard or Dijon-style French mustard. I will be doing injustice to my race if I don't suggest Bengali kashundi. It's sharp and tart, works brilliantly as a sauce, a dressing and in gravies. Unfortunately, it's only available in Kolkata and a few select shops in the metros, but if there's enough demand, supply will rush to fill the vacuum. Worth asking for a bottle if anyone's visiting Kolkata.

Oil pourer: This is a cork stopper with a metal tip for oil bottles. I find them extremely useful, especially while making mayonnaise or a salad dressing. On a daily basis, it gives a professional swirling action even if you're frying an egg.

Oils: Oils in Indian kitchens are extremely underrated. In some misinformed quest for health, most people use one standard, sanitised, flavourless variety which is often sunflower or safflower or some other polyunsaturated un-fun oil. I use one too for deep-frying or daily cooking, but the stars of my kitchen are mustard, sesame and expensive, cold-pressed, extra virgin olive that are so irresistible that I eat them raw in dressings.

Oyster sauce: A simple spinach stir-fry can become spectacularly Asian with a few splashes of oyster sauce. Versatile genius.

Salad spinner: I cannot overstate the importance of a salad spinner, if you desire restaurant-quality salads. My theory on the simplest foods (like salad) is that they need the best ingredients and technique. The most critical attributes of a salad are crispness and freshness. In order to have the first attribute, the salad leaves need to be washed in very cold water so that they are slightly petrified and then spun like crazy for them to lose all the moisture but retain the crispness. You can try kitchen towels or drip-drying, but to meet both qualities, you have to eat the salad immediately after a wash and dry, followed by quick dressing. I bought mine in a shop in Surat for Rs 99. It's made in China and the Gujaratis use the perforated bowl to soak grains and pulses for sprouting. It's convenient because it can be soaked, drained and spun dry in the same container.

Silicone whisk: I could have stopped at 'whisk' but used the silicone because it does serve a purpose greater than showing off. When we whisk various ingredients, it's often important to maintain low temperature in order to prevent curdling. Metal, being a good conductor, heats up quickly in the whisking motion and you need to break often to bring the heat down. Silicone, on the other hand…

Soy sauce: While Chinese soy sauces are used more for cooking (often as a salt substitute), it's the Japanese ones, which I can drink out of a glass. Just pour some into a small bowl and eat with steamed fish or seafood. It's light in texture, rich in flavours, healthy and simple. The most common brand is Kikkoman. A splash of it and a miracle is born.

Stock: A much recommended DIY that makes a difference to the result. While I have grown up with simmering pots of aromatic liquids through winter afternoons, I have cut down the process by replacing cooking in the plain old pot with a pressure cooker – much easier in extracting the juices of meats and vegetables to infuse the liquid. The most common stock I make is chicken – I use the bones and giblets of one bird in 4 litres of water, along with salt, pepper, one whole onion (or leek), celery, carrots, and 2 bay leaves for 45 minutes on low heat once the cooker has reached full pressure.

Steamer: This is such a civilised thing to have in the kitchen – meets all the criteria and purpose of this chapter – it's not some vainglorious vessel. I always wanted a bamboo steamer that one can place simply on a wok to steam vegetables, fish, momos, and those elegant banana leaf-wrapped things. Instead, I spotted a stainless steel one, which is even better. There's no difference in the quality of steaming and much easier to clean.

Tahini: This thick, ground sesame paste is originally West Asian and used widely in dips like hummus and babaganoush or by itself spread on toast. I dilute it with water, lime juice and some sugar and use it as a dressing for a cool cucumber salad that becomes exotic; or with soupy wheat noodles and spring onions. It is easily available and exquisite.

Tongs: When you're struggling to turn a delicate piece of fish or a barely formed shammi kabab with the not so deft spatula, visualise professional chefs with their preferred instrument – the tong. Keeps things intact.

Vinegars: Aged balsamic, cider, Chinese/Japanese rice: the term vinegar for wine that is off is offensive in the face of these world-class babies. The aged balsamic is like treacle – it does amazing things to salads and fruit like strawberries with castor sugar. Cider vinegar stands out for its tang in a dressing, and the delicate rice vinegar adds subtle but heady flavours to milder East Asian food. Plus they have exotic names like mirin.

Vodka (in the freezer): If you care for vodka, the freezer is the only place to store it. Pouring the viscous liquid into a glass is salvation for a thirsty soul.

Wine sleeve: If you like to drink a red wine outdoors on a beautiful evening or carry a bottle for a picnic, the wine sleeve is for you. It's like a life jacket for a wine bottle. When it's not on duty, it stays in the freezer, cooling the liquid within its lining. When you're ready to take your bottle for an outing, stuff it through the cylindrical hole to keep it cool.

cool kitchen essentials

Index

Beverages

Cinnamon tea 117
Garlic chhaas 118
Irish coffee 131
Lemongrass tea 116
Vanilla coffee 130

Breads, Sandwiches and Buns

Basic Bruschetta 2
Brie and honey on melba toast 19
Calcutta club chicken sandwiches 77
Cheese, mustard and onion sandwich 75
Chicken and wasabi buns 10
Club chilli cheese toast 15
Farewell chicken sandwich 76
Fat girl gone crazy: fried potato and bacon on white bread 83
Garlic pao 53
Hot chilli pork in a bun 11
Melba toast 7
Politically-incorrect chilli cheese toast 16
Prince of good times' bacon butty 91
Roasted garlic squeezed on toast 89
Shami sandwich 9

Cheese

Boursin and bhakri 17
Brie and honey on melba toast 19
Cheese, mustard and onion sandwich 75
Club chilli cheese toast 15
Fresh figs and Gorgonzola 18
Grilled haloumi 17
Politically-incorrect chilli cheese toast 16
Rocket and Parmesan salad 33

Chicken

Calcutta club chicken sandwiches 77
Chicken and wasabi buns 10
Chicken curry 101 28
Chicken stew 48
Cold noodles with vegetables and chicken in a sesame sauce 31
Dark, aromatic chicken curry 50
Farewell chicken sandwich 76
Khowswey 24

Cocktails

Bloody Mary 123
Caipirinha 120
Cosmopolitan 122
Dirty martini 122
Dry martini 121
Sangria 119

Desserts

Caramel custard 125
Chocolate fondant 126
Orange almond cake 128
Phirni (Rice custard) 124
Stewed pears in red wine 129

Dips and toppings

A version of guacamole 14
Basic party dip 13

Bruschetta toppings

- *Bacon and potato topping* 6
- *Boiled egg bhurji topping* 5
- *Mushrooms topping* 5
- *Roasted bell pepper topping* 3
- *Runny eggs topping* 4
- *Tomato & basil topping* 3

Hot and sour dip 14
Tapenade 14

Eggs

Eastern egg curry and bread 73
Egg, bacon and shrimp fried rice 79
Egg, green pea and spring onion fried rice 80

Egg-white omelette with herbs and celery 110
Egg-white omelette with mushroom and garlic 111
Eggy pasta 71
Masala egg-white omelette 112
Scrambled eggs with spring garlic 90
Toast soldiers and egg 74

Lentils and Legumes

Bengali moong dal 64
Boiled green moong dal 101
Boiled masoor dal with onions and a glug of mustard oil 100
Dressy moong dal 66
Garlic, tomato and garlic dal 70
Garlic kadhi 42
Gota shedho (Boiled whole vegetables in black gram) 94
Hummus 15
Kadhi 86
Meatball khichudi 58
Palak dal (Spinach with moong dal) 99
Sexed-up leftover dal 68
Soul masoor dal 65
Tadka (Spicy whole moong) 102

Mutton, Beef and Pork

Beef and lettuce wraps 21
Cheese and spinach pork with red chillies 38
Easy pork vindaloo 37
Egg, bacon and shrimp fried rice 79
Fat girl gone crazy: fried potato and bacon on white bread 83
Hot chilli pork in a bun 11
Meatball khichudi 58
Naga-style pork raja mirchi 26
Prince of good times' bacon butty 91
Shami kabab 8
Shami sandwich 9
Steak in minutes 54
Sunday mutton curry with potatoes 44
Wintry sausage and mustard pasta 32

Pasta

Cold noodles with vegetables and/or chicken in a sesame sauce 31
Eggy pasta 71
Pasta with basil and tomato 34
Penne with pumpkin, onion, basil and pine nuts 36
Wintry sausage and mustard pasta 32

Rice

Egg, bacon and shrimp fried rice 79
Egg, green pea and spring onion fried rice 80
Fried rice 78
Jhaal mudi (Spicy puffed rice snack) 113
Meatball khichudi 58
Mushroom and fried onion rice 82
South Indian fried rice 81

Salads and Relishes

Apple, celery and rocket salad in a blue cheese dressing 109
Caesar salad 107
Cucumber salad 53
Gado gado 40
Greek salad 108
Kachumbar (Minced onion, tomato and cucumber salad) 29
My house salad 35
Rocket salad 106
Rocket and Parmesan salad 33
Rocket and tomato salad 55
South Indian raita 51

Seafood

Egg, bacon and shrimp fried rice 79
Fried fish 46
Mustard fish 101 56
Prawn balchao 52
Prawn cocktail 7
Steamed shrimp 20

Soup

Chicken soup 84
Chicken tea soup 30

Vegetables

Aubergine
Aubergine in a garlic-yogurt sauce 60
Baingan and garlicky yogurt bharta 104
Baingan bharta 101 104
Basic baigan bharta 103
Masala baingan bharta 105

Bitter gourd
Boiled bitter gourd 97

Green peas
Egg, green pea and spring onion fried rice 80
Sautéed spinach with green peas and garlic 98

Leafy greens
Palak dal (Spinach with moong dal) 99
Sautéed spinach with green peas and garlic 98
Soupy greens 26

Mixed vegetables
California green curry 61
Cold noodles with vegetables 31
Gota shedho (Boiled whole vegetables in black gram) 94
Vegetable stew 49
Vegetarian khowswey 25

Mushroom
Egg-white omelette with mushroom and garlic 111
Mushroom and fried onion rice 82

Okra
Boiled okra 96
Masala bhindi (Spiced okra) 43

Onion
Boiled masoor dal with onions and a glug of mustard oil 100
Cheese, mustard and onion sandwich 75
Egg, green pea and spring onion fried rice 80
Mushroom and fried onion rice 82
Penne with pumpkin, onion, basil and pine nuts 36

Potato
Alu chhenchki (Potato sauté) 88
Boiled and mashed potato 96
Chilli potatoes 12
Fat girl gone crazy: fried potato and bacon on white bread 83
French fries or finger chips 47
SSpicy potatoes 87
Mashed potatoes 55
Sleep-inducing potato and poppy seeds 72

Pumpkin
Boiled pumpkin 95
Penne with pumpkin, onion, basil and pine nuts 36

Radish
Boiled radish 97

index 141

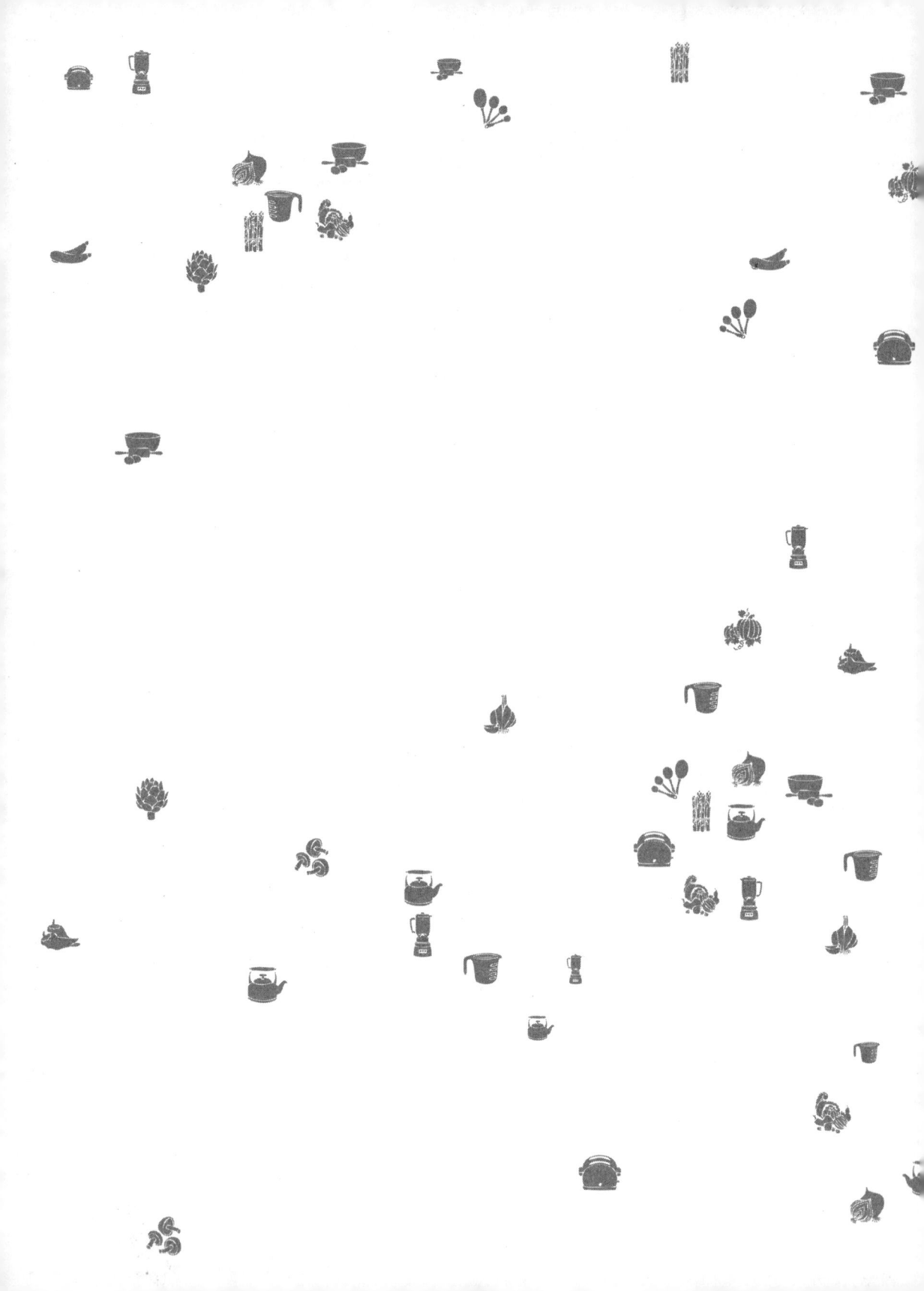